THE KINGS & QUEENS OF
ENGLAND

ROBERT J. PARKER

AMBERLEY

ABOUT THE AUTHOR

Robert Parker lives in Valparaiso, Indiana, just outside of Chicago, Illinois. He teaches history at high school and college level, holding a BA degree from Indiana University and a master's degree from Valparaiso University. He is a frequent visitor to the United Kingdom, although his travels have taken him to over seventy nations and all fifty states in the US. He has written numerous articles on British kings, queens, and prime ministers, and is the author of *British Prime Ministers* (also published by Amberley), a brief review of every British Prime Minister, dating back to Robert Walpole. He lives with his wife Sheila and son Robbie.

Previous page: 1. An Allegory of the Tudor Succession. *Introduction:* 2. Henry VIII by Hans Holbein.

Amberley Publishing
The Hill, Stroud
Gloucestershire, GL5 4EP

www.amberley-books.com

British Library Cataloguing in Publication Data.
A catalogue record for this book is available from the British Library.

ISBN 978 1 4456 1497 7 (paperback)
ISBN 978 1 4456 1500 4 (ebook)

Typeset in 10pt on 12pt Minion Pro.
Typesetting and Origination by Amberley Publishing.
Printed in the UK.

CONTENTS

INTRODUCTION

The kings of England rose from tribal chieftains to monarchs of an imperial empire that straddled the globe. Much of this accomplishment was attained because of their personalities, but much was achieved in spite of them. The men and women who have occupied the throne have been a rich and varied collection of unique, eccentric, and dominating individuals. Events in history would have occurred with or without them, but in many instances, the events were shaped and forged by the will and conduct, for better or worse, of the individual character of a particular monarch. To paraphrase Arthur Balfour, British Prime Minister (1902–1905) and would-be philosopher, 'No monarchs mattered very much and very few mattered at all.' Yet no one can doubt the powerful impact upon history of the oversized egotism of Henry VIII; the dramatic, inspirational presence of Elizabeth I; or the foolish stubbornness of Charles I. England's royal monarchs set a pattern for religious reformation, constitutional representative government, and globe-girdling empire building. In many instances it was the monarch that inspired, induced, or accelerated the events that have brought all of us to our historical present and in our current political configuration – of that there can be little denial.

Where does one begin when tracing the history of the British monarchs? This has always been a thorny question for any historian, be they professional or amateur. Likewise, a guidebook describing these personalities, whether brief or encyclopedic in length, faces the same dilemma – where to begin? The deeper one recedes into history, the scantier the information becomes, until there is nothing remaining beyond fragments and myths. We have the impressive monolithic hunks of rock at Stonehenge but no written word. We have foggy accounts of early Celtic tribal inhabitants that predate the Roman conquest, followed by several centuries of fairly well-documented Roman rule. As the Romans withdrew, replaced by repeated migrations of Angles, Saxons and Jutes, the legends of such heroic figures as King Arthur begin to emerge from the misty depths of the Dark Ages.

Out of this tangle of mixed groups, petty chieftains, and rival realms appear a group of seven minor kingdoms conveniently known as the Heptarchy. Not always seven, and very fluid in their composition, they were listed as far back as the Venerable Bede's *History of the English Church and People* (672–

735), and although not precise in its descriptions and histories, this does offer a starting point for any historical study. These seven Anglo-Saxon kingdoms began to embrace Christianity, acknowledge a local king, and establish an elementary foundation for the future attempts at unification of a single kingdom.

These seven kingdoms of the early Middle Ages are eventually going to form the Kingdom of England. They are usually identified as Wessex, Mercia, Northumbria, Sussex, East Anglia, Essex, and Kent. There were certainly other minor kingdoms, and the historical label and term 'Heptarchy' is currently out of favour, but it does serve to identify an area, a set of competing kingdoms, and eventually a dominant realm that will gain ascendancy; that being Wessex and its prominent kings. And so, in order to anchor our review in some appropriate safe haven, we turn to Egbert, King of Wessex (r. 802–839), and we begin our rediscovery of kings and queens with him, as he is frequently endowed with the designation 'first King of England'.

EGBERT

Born:	*c. 770*
Died:	839
Reigned:	802–839
Parents:	Ealhmund of Kent, mother unknown
Married:	Redburga, a Frankish queen (disputed)
Children:	Aethelwulf, and perhaps others

Egbert, King of Wessex, is often recognised as the first king of the entity 'England', although there is certainly a case for others, such as Alfred the Great, to hold that distinction. Wessex, under Egbert's leadership, assumed the position of dominant kingdom, thereby uniting the former numerous petty kingdoms of Northumbria, Mercia, etc., under one king. Egbert began an Anglo-Saxon dynasty which endured for close to 200 years and established Winchester as his most important city. Egbert would be buried in its cathedral along with numerous descendants of the early English royalty. Among the many royal descendants of Egbert who would become king were his son, Aethelwulf; four of his grandsons, including Alfred the Great; and his great-grandson Edward the Elder.

Many specifics are unknown concerning Egbert and his family, however it is believed he was exiled for a time to France and Charlemagne's Frankish empire, and perhaps married a Frankish princess. Returning to Britain, Egbert rallied support and established Wessex as the dominant region of Britain. The spread of Wessex supremacy culminated in the Battle of Ellendune, in Wiltshire, and Egbert's victory over Beornwulf, King of Mercia (825). Egbert went on to seize Mercia, take control of London, and control all of Britain south of the Humber River. From this point on, Egbert claimed and was recognised as king of an area comprising most of Britain, and his heirs were accepted by the Christian Church as the rightful line of rulers. Egbert granted lands and favours to the Church, in return for the Church's acknowledgement of his family's royal prominence. Under Egbert's administration, silver coins were minted and circulated, reflecting the strength and confidence of the Wessex king.

Near the end of his reign the Viking threat was becoming more pronounced, a condition that was to plague Britain over the next 200 years. The vicious, violent and relentless raids were evolving into fully fledged invasions and would eventually lead to Viking kings supplanting the Anglo-Saxons as monarchs, and large swaths of Britain being conquered.

Egbert died in 839 and was buried in Winchester Cathedral. His son, Aethelwulf, inherited the throne, having already ruled jointly for several years with his father.

AETHELWULF

Born:	*c.* 795
Died:	858
Reigned:	839–858
Parents:	King Egbert and (?)
Married:	(1.) Osburga and (2.) Judith of Flanders, daughter of Holy Roman Emperor Charles the Bald, King of the Franks and grandson of Charlemagne
Children:	(1.) Five sons – Aethelstan, Aethelbald, Aethelbert, Aethelred, Alfred (the Great), and one daughter – Aethelswith.

Aethelwulf (meaning 'noble wolf') followed his father Egbert as King of Wessex. Aethelwulf had gained experience by ruling jointly with his father over the last few years of Egbert's reign. His reign, and that of his sons, was dominated by the increasingly large and ever more frequent invasions of the Vikings from Scandinavia. He gave his eldest son, Aethelstan, authority over the eastern half of his kingdom while keeping the western half for himself. Aethelstan died before his father, preventing him from becoming king of what was now being considered a unified English kingdom. All four other sons of Aethelwulf became king, the youngest being Alfred – who would become 'the Great'.

To further ensure the continuity of the combined kingdoms of England, Aethelwulf had his daughter, Aethelswith, marry King Burgred of Mercia, although it was understood that Wessex would remain the dominant power of the union. All of England was suffering under the violence of incessant Viking raids, and co-operation was essential for the survival of the Saxon kingdoms.

Aethelwulf took his Christian religion quite seriously, visiting Rome and the church of St Peter in 855–856. While there he made handsome donations of gold plate to the church and its clergy. It was on the return to England that he met and married Judith, the daughter of Charles the Bald, King of the Franks and grandson of Charlemagne. Earlier, in 853, Aethelwulf had sent his youngest son, Alfred, to study in Rome.

Aethelwulf's journey to Rome tempted and encouraged his son Aethelbald to make a bid at claiming the crown for himself. Aethelwulf resolved the rebellion of Aethelbald by granting him control of over half of Wessex. The bigger worry continued to be the Viking marauders. The constant invasions and threats of attack by the Vikings were beginning to overwhelm much of England.

Aethelwulf died in 858, and was initially buried at Steyning, West Sussex, where Aethelwulf's original tombstone can still be found. Later, he was reinterred at Winchester Cathedral. His wife Judith then married Aethelbald, however they had no children and the marriage was annulled.

AETHELBALD

Born:	*c.* 831
Died:	860
Reigned:	858–860
Parents:	Aethelwulf and Osburga
Married:	Judith of Flanders, daughter of Holy Roman Emperor Charles the Bald, King of the Franks
Children:	None

Aethelbald was the second son of Aethelwulf and inherited the throne of Wessex in 858 upon the death of his father. Earlier, while his father was visiting Rome in 855–856, it is believed that Aethelbald had attempted to seize the crown for himself. Perhaps Aethelbald feared he would lose his inheritance of Wessex, since his father, on returning from his trip to Rome, had taken a young new bride, Judith of Flanders. Aethelwulf avoided conflict by allowing Aethelbald to continue ruling half of Wessex. This action prevented a civil war and the two ruled as virtual joint kings until Aethelwulf's death in 858.

Aethelbald then proceeded to marry his former stepmother, Judith, an act that raised many eyebrows and much criticism. It also probably tarnished Aethelbald's reputation in any future histories, since the histories were generally written by the clergy, and this marriage was viewed by the Church as incestuous. Either way, the marriage was childless and then annulled. Judith went on to marry Baldwin of Flanders, thus becoming an ancestress of William the Conqueror's consort!

During Aethelbald's short reign, the Viking invasions continued with greater frequency and success. The future of Anglo-Saxon England was in considerable jeopardy with no salvation in sight. Aethelbald died in 860 and was buried at Sherborne Abbey, Dorset. His brother, Aethelbert, who succeeded him as king, is also buried in the abbey.

4

AETHELBERT

Born:	836
Died:	865
Reigned:	860–865
Parents:	Aethelwulf and Osburga
Married:	Believed to have never married
Children:	Most sources believe none

Aethelbert, meaning 'magnificent noble', became King of Wessex upon the death of his older brother, Aethelbald, in 860. One of Aethelwulf's four sons to reign as king, Aethelbert had served as a petty king of Kent following the death of another older brother, Aethelstan, in 858. However, Aethelbert chose not to replace this position with a new appointment, reflecting the increased sense of a single 'England' dominated by Anglo-Saxon Wessex, under one crown.

Like his father and brother before him, Aethelbert was crowned at Kingston-upon-Thames. His reign was plagued, as were those of his father and brothers, by the continued and relentless invasions of the Vikings. Though at times temporarily halted, the Viking incursions were only growing larger and stronger. The sacking and burning of the Wessex capital of Winchester was but an early prelude to the Viking conquest and occupation of York and much of north-eastern England by 866.

Aethelbert died in 865 and was buried at Sherborne Abbey, Dorset, beside his older brother Aethelbald. Without a wife or children as heirs, his younger brother Aethelred succeeded him.

AETHELRED

Born:	*c.* 837
Died:	871
Reigned:	865–871
Parents:	Aethelwulf and Osburga
Married:	Wulfthryth (?)
Children:	At least two sons, Aethelhelm and Aethelwold
Illustration:	3. A page from Aethelred's pact with the Vikings

Aethelred, meaning 'noble counsel', was the third of Aethelwulf's sons to become King of Wessex. He succeeded his older brother Aethelbert in 865, and, as his brothers before and after, invested much time and energy attempting to resist the ruthless terror of the Vikings.

Danish Viking invasions became so extensive that in Northumbria the Norsemen were not only raiding, but occupying and settling great tracts of land north of the Humber River. Viking Ivar the Boneless led a Danish 'Great Army' that occupied York and was preparing to invade Mercia unless tribute was paid to temporarily prevent their further incursion into central England. The recently combined kingdoms formed under the Saxon leadership of Egbert and his descendants were now beginning to disintegrate under the rampaging Vikings.

By 871 the Vikings had penetrated into East Anglia and continued into Wessex, inflicting a major defeat upon Aethelred at Reading. Helping Aethelred engage the Vikings was his younger brother Alfred, who would later take centre stage as the future King Alfred the Great. But for now the Viking tide of conquest went on unabated. In the spring of 871, following a series of Viking engagements, Aethelred died, probably from wounds suffered in battle. He was only thirty-four. He was buried at Wimborne Minster, Dorset.

Although Aethelred had two young sons, Saxon rule decreed that the next king should be the most fit and able to lead the kingdom, and clearly the children were too young for such an obligation. Alfred, then, became king, and set about the stemming of the Viking onslaught.

ALFRED THE GREAT

Born:	c. 849
Died:	26 October 899
Reigned:	871–899
Parents:	Aethelwulf and Osburga
Married:	Ealhswith
Children:	At least three sons, including Edward the Elder of Wessex and Aethelweard of Wessex, and three daughters – Ethelfleda of Mercia, Aethelgifu of Wessex, and Aelfthryth of Flanders.
Illustration:	4. Detail from a painting showing Alfred the Great

The only 'English' monarch to be proclaimed 'the Great', Alfred, King of Wessex, brought security and unity to much of Britain through the stemming of the Danish Viking invasions during the ninth century. Coins and charters began referring to Alfred as 'King of the English', and so with that application begins what many consider the 'true' birth of the English monarchy. Along with the aforementioned Egbert, Alfred's significant and prominent reign set the future direction that British history would follow.

Due to Alfred's ninth-century biographer Bishop Asser, we have an extensive record of Alfred's life and achievements, far better indeed than that of any other English king up to William the Conqueror. As one of several sons of King Aethelwulf of Wessex, Alfred was sent to Rome twice, in 853 and 855, to study and enrich his scholarly interests while receiving instruction on Christianity from Pope Leo IV. Therefore, Alfred's reputation for accomplishment rests on the twin successes of resisting and settling the invading Danish Vikings while simultaneously pursuing the restoration of culture and learning – not just by decree, but by strong example.

First and foremost the Wessex kings were required to be commanders and warriors. For a century, Danish Viking invasions had been ruthlessly overrunning more and more of Anglo-Saxon England. After absorbing initial defeats and setbacks, Alfred revised Anglo-Saxon military tactics, which helped inspire both his subjects and his West Saxon allies. Alfred's leadership led his army to decisively defeat the Danes at the Battle of Edington in 878, leading to a treaty with the Danish King Guthrum. Further successful military campaigns by Alfred consolidated his position, and coupled with the strengthening of Anglo-Saxon defences and fortifications, led to the establishment of the Danelaw. The Danelaw secured separate kingdoms and sets of laws for the settled Danes in northern and eastern England, and the Anglo-Saxons of Wessex and Mercia in central and western England. More importantly, it brought a period of relative peace and stability to the island and an interruption to the violent Viking raids that had plagued England for over a century. Each kingdom would be required to enforce its laws, maintain peace, and respect its neighbouring kingdom, while coincidentally encouraging the

Christianisation of its population. In the process, Danish King Guthrum became a Christian and King Alfred his godfather.

This was not to be the end of Viking incursions into England; the struggle would continue until the mid-eleventh century. Danish King Canute would resume control of England (1016–1035), followed by a brief return of Anglo-Saxon monarchs. Eventually, English King Harold Godwinson's defeat of Harald Hardrada's large Norwegian invasion force in 1066 would conclude the last major attempt of a Viking invasion. Norman and Viking descendant William the Conqueror, however, would successfully invade England and defeat Harold Godwinson, marking the final chapter in this saga.

With this foundation of internal security, progress on cultural and social levels became possible. Alfred invited foreign scholars to establish centres of learning, he encouraged literacy among his members of court and governmental administrators (remember, this was the tail end of the European Dark Ages), and he reformed the legal codes of his kingdom. His determined interest in scholarship included his personally translating numerous Latin writings into the vernacular and encouraging the use of English in reading and writing – a movement several centuries ahead of its time. Alfred's travels in Europe throughout the Carolingian Empire, and the recognition of the achievements of former Emperor Charlemagne, no doubt inspired many of his forward-looking desires for education and reform.

Legendary stories about Alfred abound. Alfred masquerading as a minstrel to spy on his Danish opponents points to his shrewd cleverness. Later, while enduring defeats at the hands of the Danish, Alfred is sheltered and scolded by a peasant woman. According to this apocryphal story, he allowed her cakes to burn while failing to properly tend to them. Of course his mind was on larger and greater matters as he contemplated the survival of his kingdom and the future of Wessex.

Retaking, rebuilding, and fortifying London, building up the English navy (earning him another nickname as 'father of the royal navy'), and employing advanced tactical thinking in terms of fortified villages linked together for mutual protection against Viking attacks – all of these reforms and innovations contributed to his success and enduring prestige.

Alfred was recognised in his own time as a wise and just ruler, and as King of the English, even if not King of all England. He earned and deserved the title 'the Great'.

5. A statue of King Alfred the Great at Winchester.

EDWARD THE ELDER

Born:	c. 875
Died:	17 July 924
Reigned:	899–924
Parents:	Alfred the Great and Ealhswith
Married:	(1.) Ecgwynn, (2.) Aelffaed and (3.) Eadgifu.
Children:	At least six sons, including (1.) Aethelstan, (3.) Edmund and Edred, all three of whom became King of England. Ten daughters, notably Edith (1.), plus perhaps as many as three others.

Edward the Elder, in the Saxon tradition, began serving as virtual co-king before the death of his father, Alfred the Great, in 899. The chore of expelling the Vikings from Wessex continued without interruption under his reign. He was helped by his older sister Aethelflaed, married to the ruler of Mercia, who was no slouch as a worthy warrior in the chore of re-establishing the Saxon rule over England south of the Humber River. If anything, Edward probably won more battles and achieved more military success against the Vikings than did his father, but less is recorded about his victories and conquests. The result, however, set the stage for Edward's oldest son, Aethelstan, to complete the task of virtually eliminating Viking control throughout most of England.

Early in his own reign, Edward had to deal with a revolt from his cousin Aethelwold, son of his uncle and former king, Aethelred. Aethelwold was defeated and killed in 903 at the Battle of Holme. Operating from strength, Edward secured his realm by continuing to drive the Vikings further north. Following the example of his father, Edward instituted a set of fortifications that linked the freshly regained territory into a secure defensive system. The boundaries set by Edward for this interlocking defensive network remain virtually intact to this day on the county map of the Midlands.

Edward had been raised in his father's court to read and write, and, as great a warrior as Edward was, he was no less an enthusiastic administrator and scholar than his father Alfred had been. Three of his sons would go on to reign as kings of England, and two of his daughters would marry into the royal families of the Franks.

Edward died while on campaign in 924. He was buried in the New Minster, Winchester, Hampshire – a church that he had founded. It is believed that his body was later moved to the now destroyed Hyde Abbey, where today a stone marker in the park north of the city marks his recognised burial place.

AETHELSTAN

Born:	895
Died:	22 October 939
Reigned:	924–939
Parents:	Edward the Elder and Ecgwynn
Married:	Never married
Children:	None
Illustration:	6. Aethelstan's empty tomb at Malmesbury Abbey

Grandson of Alfred the Great and son of Edward the Elder, two of England's greatest medieval warriors, Aethelstan only further embellished the reputation of his forebears with a resounding victory over a Norse, Scottish and Irish coalition at the Battle of Brunanburh in 937. This victory had followed Aethelstan's re-taking of the Danish Viking stronghold of York and the territory of Northumbria, and gave him the undisputed title of King of all England. Capitalising upon his success at Brunanburh, Aethelstan then secured Scotland, leading to his further claim as King of all Britain. Though others had been acknowledged as great kings and claimed these titles, it was Aethelstan who actually achieved this accomplishment, laying his claim to being perhaps the greatest of the Anglo-Saxon warrior-kings.

Not only was Aethelstan a great and successful warrior, but he was also famous for his administration of law and refinement of the legal code, tempering punishment with justice – reflecting his practical sense of judicious consideration. Aethelstan continued Alfred the Great's emphasis on inviting scholars into his court, and he projected enthusiasm for books, learning, and the arts. He also personally participated in the promotion and collection of finely crafted jewellery, coins and relics, and it is Aethelstan who is the first King of England to be depicted wearing a golden crown. Internationally, England's growing prowess and importance was clearly demonstrated by Aethelstan's relationship with Continental Europe. Aethelstan not only communicated with fellow European royal families, but generously exchanged gifts of great value. One of his sisters married Otto the Great, Emperor of the Holy Roman Empire; and for a while Louis IV, King of the Franks, took refuge in England under Aethelstan's protection.

Aethelstan's accomplishments, though not as well-documented or as romanticised as his grandfather Alfred the Great's, give evidence as to what some refer to as an Anglo-Saxon 'Golden Age'. More than just a great Saxon warrior, Aethelstan presided over the first complete political unification of Great Britain. He was a dedicated devotee of efficient centralised administration, and held a genuine respect for learning and the arts.

Aethelstan never married or fathered any known children – perhaps due to a deep sense of religious piety. He died in Gloucester in 939 and was buried at his request in Malmesbury Abbey, Wiltshire. His bones were lost at the time of the Reformation, but an empty tomb with accompanying effigy can still be viewed. He was succeeded by his half-brother Edmund.

EDMUND I

Born:	921
Died:	26 May 946
Reigned:	939–946
Parents:	Edward the Elder and Eadgifu
Married:	(1.) Elgiva and (2.) Aethelfleda
Children:	(1.) Two sons, future kings of England Eadwig and Edgar, and one daughter.
Illustration:	7. Edmund I

Edmund, known as the 'deed-doer', was only eighteen when he became king on the death of Aethelstan, his half-brother. Another strong and resourceful Saxon warrior, by 944 Edmund had recaptured the Midlands, York, and Northumbria from the pesky Danish Norse Vikings who had temporarily recovered control. He went on to conquer south-western Scotland in 945, then cleverly turned it over to Malcom I, King of the Scots, thereby enlisting a loyal ally while protecting his northern borders.

Edmund installed Dunstan as Abbot of Glastonbury and supported the revival of monasticism. Edmund would later be buried at Glastonbury. Edmund had two sons and a daughter from his first wife, Elgiva, who died in 944 during childbirth. Both sons would go on to become kings of England.

During his brief reign Edmund was popular, dynamic and energetic. His reign was cut short in 946 when he was murdered at a banquet in Pucklechurch, Gloucestershire. A known outlaw, Liofa, was recognised in the crowd. In the attempt to apprehend the intruder, Edmund was mortally stabbed in the stomach. His sons being too young to ascend the throne, Edmund was replaced by his brother, Edred.

EDRED

Born: 923
Died: 23 November 955
Reigned: 946–955
Parents: Edward the Elder and Eadgifu
Married: Never married
Children: None
Illustration: 8. Edred

Like his brother Edmund, Edred had a short reign and a short life. Unlike his robust brother, Edred was a chronically sick man from an unspecified illness, possibly a digestive ailment. Edred never married, which may also have been due to his physical condition, and had no children. Nevertheless, Edred was another strong warrior, carrying on the successful tradition of his family. In his brief reign he accomplished the task of defeating the Norse leader of York, Eric Bloodaxe, and once again reasserting Saxon control over Northumbria. Bloodaxe, a former King of Norway and notorious for his ruthless violence, was later ambushed and killed in 954.

Edred was concerned about future Viking raids and, like his forebears, made concerted efforts to strengthen the interlinked *burhs* (boroughs). These fortified settlements were essential in providing defence against the ever-present threat of renewed Danish-Norse invasion. Edred retained many of his brother's administrators and elevated Dunstan, Abbott of Glastonbury, to be his chief minister. Edred also continued Dunstan's and his brother's policy of supporting a revived monastic movement throughout England.

The practically invalid Edred died in Frome, Somerset, at the age of only thirty-two. He was buried in the Old Minster of Winchester, today Winchester Cathedral, where his bones rest today. At the time of his death, he was perhaps the first true king of a *unified* England. He was succeeded in 955 by his nephew Eadwig.

EADWIG

Born:	*c.* 941
Died:	1 October 959
Reigned:	955–959
Parents:	Edmund I and Elgiva
Married:	Elfgifu (annulled)
Children:	None
Illustration:	9. Eadwig

Much mystery surrounds the short life of Eadwig, son of Edward the Elder, who in 955 became king at the tender age of about fourteen. The untimely early deaths of his two uncles left the crown to land upon the youthful head of Eadwig. His reign got off to a rocky start when, according to later histories, it was claimed that during his coronation feast he took time out of the festivities to engage himself with a young lady (or perhaps two!). He was interrupted from his escapade by Dunstan, the Abbot of Glastonbury and former chief administrator of the previous king, Edred. Eadwig later married the aforementioned young lady, Elfgifu, his stepmother Aethelfleda's daughter. This brought on the wrath of the Archbishop of Canterbury and the marriage was subsequently annulled before it could bear any children.

More political turmoil followed as disgruntled Northern nobles granted Eadwig's younger brother, Edgar, kingship over territory north of the River Thames, leaving Eadwig the rump south of it. Abbot Dunstan fled to the Continent, again perhaps for political reasons, and would not return until after Eadwig's death, which came soon in 959, before he had reached the age of twenty.

How much of this obscure history was true, and how much was conjured up by his political enemies who followed him, remains unclear. Also unknown is the cause or the circumstances of Eadwig's early death. What is clear is the peaceful succession by Edgar and his peaceful and stable reign as king of a single reunified England.

EDGAR

Born: 942
Died: 8 July 975
Reigned: 959–975
Parents: Edmund I and Elgiva
Married: (1.) Aethelfleda and (2.) Aelfrida
Children: At least three sons: (1.) Edward II (the Martyr, later king), (2.) Edmund and Aethelred II (later king), and one illegitimate daughter.
Illustration: 10. The coronation of King Edgar

Edgar had been declared king of the territory north of the Thames, plus Mercia and Northumbria, during the reign of his older brother Eadwig. Upon the death of Eadwig in 959, Edgar assumed the crown as King of all England. His reign was remarkably peaceful and successful, providing over a decade of relative peace and stability. Following Edgar's reign and for nearly the next century, England would suffer frequent turmoil, invasions, and occupations culminating in the Norman Conquest of 1066.

Edgar, in Saxon meaning 'rich in spears', became King of England at the age of seventeen. Even at this young age he was welcomed as a necessary improvement over the weak and imprudent Eadwig, who clearly was not favoured by either the Church or the powerful families of nobles. Edgar brought back Dunstan, the exiled former Abbot of Glastonbury. Dunstan had been removed from power and chased to the Continent by Eadwig, but Edgar returned him to a high position within his administration as principal advisor, and later saw to his appointment as Archbishop of Canterbury. This ushered in a reform of the English monasteries that more closely paralleled the monastic movement as practiced in France and elsewhere on the Continent. England's existing military security provided relaxation from fresh Norse Danish invasions, allowing building programs to extensively rebuild monasteries that had been damaged or destroyed during the previous decades of wanton Viking destruction.

Edgar was never the warrior that his Saxon forebears had been, but he did understand the power of authority. In 973, in the town of Chester, Edgar arranged for six kings of Britain, including those of Wales and Scotland, to row him on a royal barge down the River Dee. This tale, whether apocryphal or not, demonstrates and underscores the image of Edgar as the acknowledged king who receives the promise of loyalty and homage from his vassals.

Earlier in 973, it was recorded that Edgar journeyed to the town of Bath for a royal coronation of great splendour and pomp. Anointed and crowned as 'King of the English', the ceremony, as conducted, became the standard for all future royal coronations in England. This coronation came late in Edgar's reign, perhaps an indication of his attaining personal maturity and acceptance as a creditable monarch. It was the first English coronation to specifically use the title 'King of the English' in the coronation ceremony. The ceremony also included the coronation of Edgar's wife Aelfrida as queen – another first.

Though praised as a monarch, Edgar also earned a reputation as a notorious rake. He married the sixteen-year-old Aethelfleda and produced a son, the future Edward II. He supposedly seduced and fathered a daughter with a nun named Wulfrith, who refused to marry him even after the death of Aethelfleda. For this action, Dunstan assigned Edgar a penance of not wearing his crown for seven years. Later, in 965, he married Aelfrida, whose first husband was killed in a 'hunting accident' – supposedly with a spear thrown by Edgar! They also produced a son who would become a king, Aethelred II. Aelfrida would later be involved in the murder of her stepson, King Edward II, providing a vacancy for her own son, Aethelred, to become king.

Edgar died in 975 at Winchester, succeeded by his eldest son Edward, and was buried in Glastonbury Abbey. Whether through Edgar's leadership abilities or his direction from a host of prudent advisors, his reign featured peace and stability. His strong support of Dunstan and the Church undoubtedly helped Edgar achieve a positive historical reputation, as many early histories were largely composed by the Church. Edgar's sixteen-year rule was to be the last successful and effective Saxon reign, as well as the last uncontested succession until after the Norman Conquest.

11. A statue of King Edgar at Powis Castle.

EDWARD II 'THE MARTYR'

Born:	*c.* 962
Died:	18 March 978
Reigned:	975–978
Parents:	Edgar and Aethelfleda
Married:	Unmarried
Children:	None
Illustration:	12. The seal of Edward II

Edward was only twelve or thirteen years old when he succeeded his father as king. The eldest son of Edgar and Edgar's first wife Aethefleda, it is believed that Edward suffered from fits of uncontrolled emotional rage. This description may or may not be correct, but in 978, Edward was induced to visit his stepmother Aelfrida and her son, his half-brother Aethelred, at Corfe Castle. The invitation for dinner turned out to be a guise to lure the unsuspecting Edward, still only fifteen years old, into a convenient situation where he could be summarily murdered. This devious plot allowed Aelfrida's own ten-year-old son, Aethelred, to become king. How much of this story is fact is subject to conjecture, but this much is certain: the elimination of Edward for the ten-year-old Aethelred was to usher in a period of great instability.

Certainly the ranking nobles at the time were the true directors of policy due to the young age of the royal heirs, and they would have been behind any manipulation of who would or would not be recognised as the rightful sovereign. Many important nobles rejected the expanded monastic policies of the young Edward, who pursued the policies of his father King Edgar and the influential Dunstan, Archbishop of Canterbury. A faction of nobles was encouraging a reduction in the power and wealth of the growing monastic movement, hence the need to remove Edward and replace him with Aethelred. Murdering a young king to achieve their goals would not be out of the question.

Edward's pro-monastic policy and violent death would also explain his elevation by the Church to sainthood and the stories of miracles attributed to his martyred bones and relics. Buried at Wareham, Dorset, his tomb soon became a shrine for pilgrims. Edward's bones were soon shifted to Shaftesbury Abbey and later honoured, ironically, by his half-brother King Aethelred II. Today, after a circuitous set of circumstances, Edward's relics and bones reside at the Eastern Orthodox Church at the Brookwood Cemetery in Surrey.

AETHELRED II 'THE UNRAED'

Born:	968
Died:	23 April 1016
Reigned:	978–1013 and 1014–1016
Parents:	Edgar and Aelfrida
Married:	(1.) Aelgifu and (2.) Emma of Normandy
Children:	(1.) Eight sons, including future King of England Edmund 'Ironside', Aelthstan, Egbert, Edred, Eadwig, Edgar, and five daughters. (2.) Two sons: future King of England Edward the Confessor, and Alfred, and one daughter, Goda
Illustration:	13. Aethelred II.

Aethelred II became King of England in 978 upon the murder of his half-brother, the fifteen-year-old Edward, at Corfe Castle. This treacherous act was probably carried out under the supervision of Aethelred's ambitious mother Aelfrida, and endorsed by powerful English earls who desired a different direction in policy. Though present, the ten-year-old Aethelred can hardly be blamed for the assassination, though it did allow his becoming king.

Aethelred means 'noble counsel', though his lack of success as king led to his being termed 'Aethelred Unraed'; 'unraed' meaning poor counsel or lacking good counsel. Later histories converted this word to 'unready', but by either term, Aethelred II's long reign as king was a failure. Much of the failure can be blamed on Aethelred's poor choice of advisors and their ill-advised counsel – hence the name.

England was again plagued by renewed and repeated Danish Viking invasions, which ended up with the conquest of the kingdom. Aethelred lacked the military prowess, ability, and leadership to defeat the Viking invaders on the battlefield, and his attempts to buy off the Vikings with expensive tribute, the Danegeld, ultimately failed. The result was wave after wave of Norse assaults upon England securing plunder and booty, eventually resulting in conquest.

Aethelred's response to military defeats and humiliating payments was to declare and encourage the massacre of Danish settlers living within England, regardless of their peaceable or loyal behaviour. This violent and irresponsible policy resulted in the killing of Danish king Sweyn Forkbeard's sister. Sweyn had previously raided England and besieged London, until being bought off with loot and cash. Aethelred's foolish reprisals against the local Danes only further enraged the Norse Danes, who, led by the vengeful Sweyn's invasion fleet, proceeded to conquer England. Sweyn was then placed on the throne of both Denmark and England. Aethelred soon fled England for Normandy, where he took refuge. His exile lasted until the death of Sweyn in 1014, allowing a nervous Aethelred to return to England. Aethelred then feebly ruled England for two more years until his own death in 1016.

Aethelred did not have the best of luck, as the Viking Danes were at this time strong in number and ambition. But Aethelred's responses and tactics were poorly planned, weak, and usually counterproductive. He failed to provide adequate leadership or policy and the result was the rule of England by a series of Danish kings well into the eleventh century.

Aethelred died in 1016, and was succeeded by his son Edmund, who was anxious to rid England of Danish rule. Edmund, a dynamic warrior, was the son of Aethelred's first wife, Aelgifu, and he proceeded to carve out a string of victories against the conquering Danes, before succumbing to an early death. Another son, Edward, from Aethelred's second wife, Emma of Normandy, would inherit the crown following the end of Danish rule. His role, as the pious Edward the Confessor, would be the pivot on which all of England's immediate and future history would hinge.

Aethelred died in London and was buried in Old St Paul's Cathedral.

SWEYN 'FORKBEARD'

Born:	960
Died:	3 February 1014
Reigned:	King of Denmark 986–1014 and King of England 1013–1014
Parents:	Harold Bluetooth and Tove (Gunhild)
Married:	(1.) Guinhelda and (2.) Sigrid
Children:	(1.) Two sons, Harald and Canute, King of England, one daughter, Estrid, and probably several more daughters with (1.) or (2.)

During the troubled reign of Aethelred II, raids and invasions upon England by the Danish Vikings again became more and more frequent, violent, and successful. Aethelred not only squandered the advantages that previous Saxon kings had laboured to develop for the defence of England against Viking attack, but further encouraged Viking wrath with his ill-advised policy of ordering the massacre of Danes who had peaceably settled in England from previous incursions. Among the victims was Gunnhild, the sister of Sweyn 'Forkbeard', King of Denmark.

Sweyn was the son of Harald Bluetooth, previous King of Denmark. Harald, Sweyn, and other Norse kings – notably Olaf of Norway, had participated in years of lucrative Scandinavian raids upon England. By 986, Sweyn had decided to oust his father from the throne, and successfully took the Crown of Denmark, and later, Norway too. In response to the Norse campaign of terror, England under Aethelred turned to the expensive expedient of paying off the Vikings in order to prevent further attacks. The problem with paying this tribute was that it encouraged renewed raids that generated increased payments. This payment, known as the Danegeld, continued from 991 to 1013 and culminated in 1013 with Sweyn's conquest of England and the temporary exile of Aethelred to the Continent.

After more than a decade of periodic plunder and extortion, Sweyn's revenge for his sister's death was fulfilled in the form of a mighty Viking invasion fleet with Sweyn at its head. Aethelred was no match for this invasion in either fighting skill or determination, and in 1013 he fled to Normandy. Sweyn was soon recognised by the Saxon nobility as their new king. Sweyn's reign, however, was short-lived. In 1014 he fell off his horse and was killed, allowing Aethelred the opportunity to return to England as king.

Sweyn's marriage to Guinhelda, and later Sigrid, produced a daughter and two sons: Harald, who became King of Denmark, and Canute, who became king of both Denmark and England. The descendants of his daughter Estrid continue to reign over Denmark to this day. There is considerable dispute over which wife produced which child, although it is generally acknowledged that Guinhelda was the mother of Harald.

Sweyn's body was returned to Denmark and buried in the cathedral at Roskilde. Two years later, Sweyn's son Canute would return to re-conquer England and reclaim the throne.

EDMUND II 'IRONSIDE'

Born:	989
Died:	30 November 1016
Reigned:	1016
Parents:	Aethelred II and Aelgifu
Married:	Eagwyth (Edith)
Children:	Two sons: Edward (the 'Exile') and Edmund
Illustration:	14. Edmund II

Edmund was everything that an English Saxon king should be, and that his father, King Aethelred II, was not: courageous, determined, and a capable military commander willing and able to defend England against the Viking threat.

Aethelred had been driven into exile by the Viking King of Denmark, Sweyn 'Forkbeard', in 1013. Sweyn then claimed the Crown of England, only to die from a fall from a horse in 1014, which brought the ineffective Aethelred back to the throne. By 1016, Aethelred and Edmund's two older brothers had died, leaving a vacuum for the crown. Edmund then began a whirlwind campaign of fighting the Norse Danes wherever and whenever he could, earning a reputation as a strong warrior and acquiring the nickname 'Ironside'.

Edmund was opposed by Sweyn's son, Canute. Another in the long line of fierce and resourceful Danish warriors, Canute had gained experience while fighting by his father's side and was now ready to challenge Edmund for control of England. Edmund had established his formidable presence by seizing control of the Danish-ruled region of England, the 'Danelaw', and defying his father by marrying a Dane, Eagwyth. Edmund was eager to reject his father's policy of paying cash tribute to the Vikings, and to defend England and resist Canute's invasion. Unfortunately, many of the English nobles, including those in Mercia, opted to support Canute and reject Edmund. This seriously weakened Edmund's position, and although he won several battles against Canute, he was defeated in 1016 at the major Battle of Ashingdon in Essex.

Edmund's position and reputation, however, remained strong. It was decided that England would be divided between Canute and Edmund, with Edmund ruling over Wessex, and Canute as King of Mercia and the Danish area north of the Thames River.

Edmund had literally worn himself out in the struggle to re-establish English supremacy and he died in 1016. Some later stories attribute his death to murder by treacherous nobles who favoured a unified peace with Canute as king. Edmund was buried at Glastonbury Abbey, but his tomb and burial location were hopelessly lost at the time of the sixteenth-century Dissolution of the Monasteries.

Edmund had two infant sons from his wife Eagwyth. Both were scheduled to be sent to Sweden and murdered by order of Canute, but they escaped that fate and ended up being safely raised in Hungary.

CANUTE

Born:	c. 995
Died:	12 November 1035
Reigned:	1016–1035
Parents:	Sweyn 'Forkbeard' and Guinhelda
Married:	(1.) Aelgifu and (2.) Emma of Normandy (widow of Aethelred II)
Children:	(1.) Two sons: Harold Harefoot, King of England, and Sweyn Knutsson. (2.) One son: Harthacanute, King of England, and two daughters: Gunhilda and one unknown, plus several (?) other illegitimate children
Illustration:	15. The charter of Canute

Canute, the Dane, became King of all England upon the death of Edmund II 'Ironside' in 1016. There was now no creditable candidate from the Saxon-controlled regions of England to challenge his dominant position as warrior and ruler. His Danish army was far and away the most powerful force in England and many English nobles had already aligned themselves with Canute during his war with Edmund. In 1017, Canute was officially crowned King of England in London's Old St Paul's Cathedral, and two years later added Denmark to his empire on the death of his brother Harald II.

Canute's connection with England began when he accompanied his father, Sweyn 'Forkbeard', King of Denmark, on his raids, and later conquest, of England. After Sweyn's death in 1013, Canute returned to Denmark and readied a massive Danish army and navy. In 1015 Canute embarked for England, engaging the formidable warrior and recently crowned King of England, Edmund II 'Ironside', for control of England. Canute's decisive victory over Edmund's forces at the Battle of Ashingdon, in 1016, brought about a mutually negotiated division of England between the two powerful warriors. But Edmund's subsequent death left Canute as the last, and strongest, king standing.

Canute had a fondness for England and spent most of his time there. He went about systematically putting it in order – in this he was ruthlessly violent and thorough. English nobles were weeded out through banishment or execution and replaced by Canute's loyal Norse cohorts. The treacherous Eadric, Earl of Mercia, who had helped undermine Edmund, and Uhtred, Earl of Northumbria, who had broken his allegiance to Canute's father, Sweyn 'Forkbeard', were both singled out for rapid execution. Any potential claimants to the throne were murdered, including Eadwy, King Aethelred II's last surviving son from his first marriage. Edmund's two sons, scheduled for execution in Sweden, managed to escape to, of all places, far-off Hungary.

Taxation was imposed and collected, laws were codified and enforced, and the kingdom was subdivided into administrative areas with Canute's trusted allies placed in control. Gradually, Canute began elevating loyal Saxons to positions of power and his rule was recognised to be beneficial in its restoration of order and security. With a Viking Dane as king, England was no longer threatened by repeated Viking raids, as Canute's command kept his fellow marauding warriors at bay.

To further reinforce his English connection, Canute gave up his first wife, Aelgifu of Northampton, and married Emma of Normandy, the widowed wife of Aethelred II. Though ten years his senior, Emma accepted a return to England as queen, and provided another heir to add legitimacy and further underscore Canute's claim as King of England. Canute's younger son from Aelgifu, Harold 'Harefoot', would later reign for five ineffective years as King of England. Their older son Sweyn would become King of Norway. 'Harefoot' would be followed by the even less effective two-year reign of Harthacanute, Canute's son from Emma and chosen heir.

Queen Emma was really quite central in the determination of who would contend for the position of, or become, a future king of England. Earlier, Emma had produced two sons from her *previous* marriage to King Aethelred II. Following Canute's death in 1035, one of these sons, Aetheling (Alfred), would attempt an invasion of England and be thwarted and murdered by one of Canute's newly trusted Saxon earls, Godwin. The other son, *supported* by Godwin, would become King Edward the Confessor – who would, along with Godwin's son Harold, figure so prominently in the Norman Conquest of 1066.

Canute's reputation among his subjects was very strong – strong to the point of lavish patronisation by the nobles serving him. But the practical Canute, realistic about his exaggerated reputation, offered a demonstration to show his nobles that his power was finite. Wading into the ocean on the beach at Bosum on the English Channel, Canute ordered the tide to be held back. Of course it wouldn't be held back, therefore offering proof to his well-intentioned but nonetheless sycophantic nobles that his kingly powers on earth, or for that matter any mortal man's, are ultimately limited, no matter his rank or station.

Besides being ruler of a large Scandinavian empire, Canute enjoyed the prestige of being a recognised European head of state. On Canute's visit to Rome, the first visit by an English king since Alfred the Great (who only visited as a boy rather than as a king), he was received by the Pope, and met with other leaders such as Conrad II, Holy Roman Emperor. They discussed and agreed upon a number of issues such as their borders in Northern Europe, Baltic trade, and the reduction of levies and tolls placed on Christian pilgrims making journeys through Europe.

Due to his enormous influence, impact, and personality, Canute is sometimes referred to as 'the Great'. A strong case could be made for this designation. Canute died at Shaftesbury, Dorset, in 1035 and was buried at the Old Minster at Winchester. Today his remains are interred in Winchester Cathedral; his bones, mixed with the bones of numerous Saxon, English, and Scandinavian monarchs of medieval England, appropriately all reside together in a chest above the altar.

HAROLD I 'HAREFOOT'

Born:	*c.* 1016
Died:	17 March 1040
Reigned:	1035–1040
Parents:	King Canute and Aelgifu of Northampton
Married:	Never
Children:	Aelfwine, an illegitimate son who reportedly became a monk

Following the death of Danish and English King Canute in 1035, a struggle for the crown between his two young sons, Harold and Harthacanute, ensued. They were born of separate mothers, who were each represented by supporting groups of nobles. A division of realms was agreed to whereby Harold would be king in the north of England, and regent in the south for his younger brother Harthacanute, who would also be King of Denmark. Eventually, Harold claimed the throne of all England, leading to Harthacanute's planned invasion of England to seize the throne from his older brother. In the event, the invasion was not necessary due to Harold's death in 1040.

Harold had been supported by his mother, Aelgifu (King Canute's first wife), and a leading noble, Earl Leofric. Later, Harold's claim was reinforced by a former ally of Harthacanute, Earl Godwin of Wessex. Both of these powerful earls would figure prominently in the succession of the English crown after the early deaths of both Harold and Harthacanute. To further solidify his position, Harold had Harthacanute's mother Emma (Canute's second wife) banished to the Continent. Harold then captured another of Emma's sons, and potential claimant to the throne, Harthacanute's stepbrother Alfred. Alfred, whose brother was to become King Edward the Confessor, died after Harold ordered his eyes to be gouged out.

Harold's nickname, 'Harefoot', supposedly stemmed from his ability to run fast. His reign was short and dominated by his mother, reflecting both his youth and weakness to rule. Harold died in Oxford, suddenly and of unknown causes. He was the first English king to be buried at Westminster Abbey, only to have his brother exhume his body, desecrate the tomb, and proceed to behead and mutilate the corpse before scattering it in the marshes of the River Thames. His mutilated remains were reportedly recovered and interred at London's St Clement the Danes church, although some suggest he was reinterred at Winchester Cathedral beside his father and brother.

If Harold Harefoot's reign was short, brutal, and ineffective, his brother's was shorter and even less successful – he deservedly earned the people's hatred and antipathy for his cruelty and high taxes.

HARTHACANUTE

Born:	1018
Died:	8 June 1042
Reigned:	1040–1042
Parents:	King Canute and Emma of Normandy
Married:	Never
Children:	None
Illustration:	16. The resting place of Harthacanute and his mother, Queen Emma

Harthacanute inherited Denmark and England from his father, King Canute. Harthacanute's mother, Emma, was considered to be more 'legitimate' than Canute's first wife, Aelgifu, who was the mother of Harold Harefoot, Harthacanute's older brother. This led to contention for the throne of England that was only resolved with the early death of Harold.

An agreement between the two half-brothers determined that Harold Harefoot would reign over northern England and serve as his brother's regent in southern England. Harthacanute would rule as King of Denmark, and eventually succeed to the Crown of England, as prescribed by King Canute's wishes. Harthacanute, with his mother Emma's backing, was intent upon uniting his claims to both Denmark and England, but was hampered in his effort to do so by a military threat upon Denmark from Magnus of Norway. In the meantime, much to Harthacanute's anger, Harold Harefoot had claimed all of England and declared himself king.

Harthacanute reached an agreement with Magnus to settle their conflict, thus allowing Harthacanute the freedom to mount an invasion of England and remove his erstwhile half-brother Harold Harefoot, whom he considered a usurper, from the throne. By the time the invasion got under way in 1040, Harold Harefoot had died, paving the way for Harthacanute to claim the crowns of both England and Denmark. A far-reaching consequence of Harthacanute's settlement with Magnus of Norway was an agreement between them concerning the event of death of either without an heir. The death of either would entitle inheritance of the other's kingdom. It was this agreement that would justify Norway's King Harald Hardrada attempting to claim the throne of England in 1066, and it would lead to his ensuing failed invasion.

Arriving in England, Harthacanute began a two-year reign of crushing taxes and violent retributions. The body of his half-brother Harold Harefoot was exhumed, beheaded, and thrown into the marshes of the River Thames. To pay for his invasion he raised taxes to such high levels that rebellion soon broke out. The town of Worcester was nearly destroyed in brutal retaliation over its bitter objection to the taxes. The legend of Lady Godiva (wife of Earl Leofric, who was responsible for the collection of the region's taxes) riding naked through the streets of Coventry in protest of the extreme taxes came from her sympathy to the complaints concerning Harthacanute's draconian measures.

Harthacanute's short, harsh, and unpopular reign came to an end with his death at a wedding reception in 1042. Most accounts attribute his death to a lethal bout of binge drinking, although some sources suggest he was slipped a cup of poison. He was only twenty-four years old. Harthacanute was buried at Winchester Cathedral beside his father, King Canute.

Harthacanute's reign provided one more lasting effect; reneging on his agreement with Magnus of Norway, Harthacanute declared his other half-brother, Edward, to be his heir. Edward was another of Emma's sons, whose father King Aethelred II was a Saxon. It was Edward's brother Alfred who had been murdered by Harold Harefoot, and it was *this* Edward who would inherit the throne of England as Edward the Confessor and restore the kingdom temporarily to Saxon rule.

EDWARD THE CONFESSOR

Born:	c. 1004
Died:	5 January 1066
Reigned:	1042–1066
Parents:	Aethelred II and Emma of Normandy
Married:	Edith, daughter of Earl Godwine of Wessex
Children:	None
Illustration:	17. Edward the Confessor

As the last surviving son of Aethelred II, Edward restored the throne of England to the House of Wessex, although in reality, Edward was more Norman than English. Edward succeeded his half-brother Harthacanute, both having the same mother, Emma of Normandy. Edward became King of England through a series of unlikely circumstances, and as king he became the person on which the fate of England would hinge.

Edward was already in his mid-forties when he assumed the throne. He was not a warrior, nor a charismatic leader, but he was a survivor. After the Viking conquest of England, he had spent most of his life in Normandy, living in exile with his mother's family. He had been protected by Emma's brother Richard II, the Duke of Normandy, and enjoyed the safety and material influences of Norman society; he never expected a return to England to become king. He was pious, peaceful, and without royal ambition.

Edward had no children, a fact that was to have enormous repercussions. Whether this was an intentional celibacy due to his piety (as many later histories claim) or infertility has been greatly debated ever since. His wife Edith was the daughter of the ruthless and treacherous Earl Godwine of Wessex. Godwine had curried favour with the Norse King of England, Canute, and received powerful appointments in return for his loyalty to the great ruling Dane. It was Godwine who was responsible for the mutilation and murder of Edward's brother Alfred. These were dangerous people to place misguided trust in, and Edward had wisely been content to remain in Normandy living a comfortably mundane life.

This situation changed with the death of one monarch or eligible heir after another, leaving Edward next in the line of succession. It was King Harthacanute, perhaps sensing a short life, who invited his half-brother Edward to return to England in 1041. The sudden and unexpected death of Harthacanute, still only in his early twenties, ushered in the coronation of Edward in 1042. Edward then reached an understanding with the powerful and treacherous Earl Godwine, an understanding that led Godwine to convince Edward to marry his daughter Edith. Edward's childless marriage, however, would require the Godwine family to resort to other means to procure the royal line of succession for their family.

Much of Edward's reputation for piety and religious sanctity was embellished after his death, when he was elevated to sainthood and bestowed with the title 'Edward the Confessor'. Certainly he did preside over a stable and prosperous realm, which allowed him to begin construction of Westminster Abbey. The abbey, begun in 1050 and dedicated in 1065, became Edward's burial site and an early English example of Norman (Romanesque) architecture. This building endured for about 200 years, being replaced in 1245 by the current Gothic-style abbey and site of today's shrine to Edward the Confessor. Nothing of the original Norman structure remains above ground. Having been canonised by the Pope in 1161, Edward was reburied in the abbey's splendid new shrine in 1269.

Edward enjoyed all things Norman, including his choice of Normans for principal administrative posts. Norman influence was particularly upsetting to Godwine, who preferred English or Danish influence, and he opposed the appointment of a Norman as Archbishop of Canterbury in 1051. By this time, Edward, allied by friendly and powerful earls, was secure enough in his position to have Godwine and his family exiled, and his own wife Edith cast into a nunnery. The ever resourceful Godwine, however, was back within a year, restoring Edith as queen and removing the Norman archbishop. Godwine's threatening presence and relentless challenge ended with his death in 1053.

The death of Edward in 1066 initiated the tumultuous events that would lead to the Norman Conquest and reign of William the Conqueror. There was, and remains, great confusion as to whom Edward selected to be heir to the throne of England. Over several years, however, the main candidates *all* believed they had received Edward's blessing, and perhaps they had. A struggle was inevitable.

Edmund Ironside's son, Edward the Exile, had been invited by Edward the Confessor to return to England and was named heir by both the Confessor and his council. However, within days of his return from Hungary in 1057, he mysteriously died – some say he was murdered by the Godwines. The Exile also had a son, Edgar, but he was very young and lacked any substantial backing in England. Edgar does reappear frequently throughout the later reign of William and lived to be at least seventy-five years old, the last in the original family line of Anglo-Saxon kings. He was never a serious contender to Edward's throne.

Harald Hardrada, a Viking King of Norway, claimed an agreement with King Harthacanute: whichever king died first, the other king would inherit the throne of England. Harold exercised this option in 1066, but was decisively defeated and killed by Harold Godwinson at the Battle of Stamford Bridge near York. Harald Hardrada was supported in his invasion by Tostig, brother of Harold Godwinson and one of five powerful noble sons of the deceased Godwine. He too was killed at Stamford Bridge, a traitor to his brother's cause.

Harold Godwinson, of the powerful and ambitious Godwine family, claimed that Edward the Confessor had declared him heir to the throne on his deathbed in January 1066. Harold was then immediately crowned King of England that same month in 1066. Harold Godwinson had been a loyal supporter of King Edward the Confessor, but supposedly he had also previously pledged his allegiance to Duke William of Normandy for the Crown of England. William expected this pledge to be honoured.

William, Duke of Normandy, based his claim to the throne on a promise in 1051 from his cousin Edward the Confessor, whom the Normans had protected during the reign of King Canute. William had also entertained Harold Godwinson after Harold had been shipwrecked in the English Channel. It was during this visit that Harold supposedly promised to acknowledge and support William's claim to the throne upon Edward the Confessor's death. In William's mind, he had been projected as heir by both Edward and Harold.

The stage was now set for the Norman Conquest of 1066. Edward the Confessor, a title bestowed upon him over a century later, died in January 1066 after a lingering illness. He was buried in his newly consecrated Norman church, Westminster Abbey. Within a year of Edward's death, Harold, followed by William, Duke of Normandy, would be crowned King of England in that very same abbey, as nearly all future monarchs of England would be.

18. Edward the Confessor as king, in a scene from the Bayeux Tapestry.

HAROLD II 'GODWINSON'

Born:	*c.* 1020
Died:	14 October 1066
Reigned:	1066
Parents:	Earl Godwine of Wessex and Gytha
Married:	(1.) Aedgyth (Edith 'Swan-neck'), unacknowledged, and (2.) Ealdgyth (Edith) of Mercia
Children:	(1.) Three sons (?), Godwine, Edmund and Magnus and two daughters (?), Gunhild and Gytha. (2.) Two sons, Harold and Ulf, and several (?) daughters
Illustration:	19. Harold II 'Godwinson' as king, in a scene from the Bayeux Tapestry

Harold Godwinson, the son of the powerful and treacherous Godwine, Earl of Wessex, was the last Anglo-Saxon King of England. He succeeded Edward the Confessor as king in January 1066, but was defeated and killed at the Battle of Hastings in October of the same year by William, Duke of Normandy.

Harold became Earl of Wessex on the death of his father in 1053. Loyal and dedicated to his brother-in-law, King Edward the Confessor, it was assumed by many that Harold would become the next king. Harold was recognised as the heir to the throne by King Edward on his deathbed in January 1066. With this blessing, coupled with the approval of the Witan (council of leading nobles), Harold, the most powerful noble in England, was crowned king in Westminster Abbey on the day of Edward's funeral.

Earlier in his career, Harold had been shipwrecked in the English Channel. He was given a safe refuge in Norman France by William, Duke of Normandy. As a gracious host, William entertained Harold with feasts, hunts, and even participation in battles. William claimed that Harold not only swore his allegiance to him at this time but acknowledged him as heir to be King of England upon the death of Edward the Confessor, a claim that Harold later denied.

In January of 1066, Harold attended the funeral of King Edward the Confessor at Westminster Abbey. Immediately following the funeral and in the same building, Harold was crowned King of England. Harold's position was soon threatened by serious rivals possessing large invasion fleets. The first came from the north, where the Viking Harald Hardrada, King of Norway, had landed near the town of York with a huge contingent of Norse warriors. Hardrada, believing that he too was entitled to the throne of England, was in alliance with Tostig, brother of Harold Godwinson. Harold Godwinson rapidly formed an Anglo-Saxon army and, through a series of forced marches, surprised Hardrada at Stamford Bridge, north of York, in September of 1066. Godwinson's forces inflicted a devastating defeat on Hardrada and his invasion force; Hardrada and Tostig were both killed, and the Norse army nearly annihilated. Before the battle, Tostig had refused his brother's offer to return to the Saxon cause.

Harold Godwinson quickly concluded a peace with the Norwegian king's son Olaf, and what was left of the shattered invasion fleet returned to Norway.

No sooner had Godwinson defeated the forces of Hardrada in the north than he received news from the south of England announcing the huge invasion fleet of William, Duke of Normandy, crossing the English Channel and arriving at the town of Hastings. Now Harold Godwinson's forced marches were conducted in reverse, this time to the south of England. Attempting to reinforce his exhausted army along the way, Harold Godwinson again conducted an amazingly rapid movement of his army and took up a strong defensive position on Senlac Hill north of the channel town of Hastings.

There has always been much debate as to why Harold chose to fight so soon. Waiting for William to march north would have, in theory, bought Harold time to allow his Saxon army to rest and to gather reinforcements. But Harold feared that William would begin building fortified castles and spread his authority over southern England, gaining momentum as he went along. It also was not in his nature to delay. Harold was an impetuous warrior and his Saxon blood was hot; he was ready and willing to do battle and settle the issue in the here and now. Plus he had a veteran army already assembled and freshly inspired by a momentous victory over Hardrada. Finally, he chose to occupy a solid defensive position and challenge William to attack his mighty 'shield wall' of lethal swords, spears, and double-bladed battleaxes.

William, though, had gauged his opponent well, and the exhausted Saxon army therefore stood its ground and awaited its fate. William and his Normans, on foreign soil and needing to march north and on to London, accepted the challenge and attacked Harold's forces in a vicious day-long orgy of blood, severed limbs, and mutilated bodies. Both armies were evenly matched in numbers, courage, and determination. The issue was in doubt until near the end of the day, when, sensing victory, the Saxons broke ranks and charged into the valley, offering the Normans the opportunity to overrun the Saxon high ground with their mounted knights. Harold was killed, probably by an axe to the head rather than an arrow to the eye, as many seem to believe the Bayeux Tapestry depicts. Harold and a host of his fellow nobles, including his two brothers Gurth and Leofwine, were all slaughtered by the conquering Normans, and little mercy was shown to those attempting a headlong escape.

The victory at Hastings was complete. What isolated and poorly led resistance remained was ruthlessly crushed by William's occupation and enforced domination. The fate of England was now to take a different turn. The blending of the Norman and Anglo-Saxon languages, cultures, and customs was to gradually evolve into a hybrid society of vast and rich potential.

Harold's body was buried in the coastal town of Pevensey, though it is widely believed that his mistress, Edith 'Swan-neck', later moved it to Waltham Abbey in Essex, which Harold had founded in 1060.

WILLIAM I 'THE CONQUEROR'

Born:	c. 1027
Died:	9 September 1087
Reigned:	1066–1087
Parents:	Robert, Duke of Normandy, and Herleva
Married:	Matilda
Children:	Four sons, including: William II (Rufus), King of England, Henry I, King of England, Robert (Curthose), Richard, and six daughters, including Adela of Blois
House:	Norman
Illustration:	20. William (left) in a scene from the Bayeux Tapestry

William was only a small boy when in 1035 his father Robert, the Duke of Normandy, died, leaving William to succeed him. He witnessed numerous examples of violence and observed the three noblemen designated to protect him all murdered. By 1047, Normandy was under attack from William's cousin Guy of Burgundy, but with the help of the French king, William and his dukedom survived. Warfare, violence and fighting would become the hallmarks of William and his personality. By the time he was in his early twenties, William was an experienced warrior with an appetite and aptitude for success on the battlefield. He would exercise both of these qualities to the fullest as he organised, orchestrated, and accomplished in 1066 the Conquest of England, becoming the King of England we know today as William the Conqueror.

William honed his leadership talents during several wars, defending and expanding his duchy. He was a physically and mentally powerful man, intensely focused and possessed of enormous energy. He was a skilled politician, shrewd negotiator, clever diplomat, and ruthless intimidator of friend and foe alike. He was savvy enough to befriend the Church in order to gain its support for his various policies, in particular his conquest of England.

In 1051 he had visited England and his cousin, King Edward the Confessor, whom he later claimed indicated a preference for William to be his heir to the throne. In 1064, William provided hospitality for Harold Godwinson when Harold was shipwrecked off the Norman coast. Again, William was to claim that Harold had accepted his claim to the English throne, along with a promise of sworn allegiance from Harold to William acknowledging that fact. Both of these promised commitments became part of the Norman history of the Conquest, yet there remains no evidence to verify the validity of either of these claims beyond William's word.

The preparation for the Channel crossing involved considerable time, expense, and logistical expertise. Although exact numbers are difficult to determine, it is generally accepted that William recruited an army of about 7,000 Norman and French soldiers; this included archers, foot soldiers, and roughly 3,000 heavily armoured knights. To move this group across the treacherous English Channel required a fleet of approximately 700 ships, each similar to the larger Viking longboats, and some capable of transporting horses, armour, and heavy equipment. Due to inclement weather, the armada was delayed a month in setting sail, an enormous challenge in terms of cost, morale, and sheer weight of provisioning. It is estimated that William had to provide a minimum of 14 tons of grain *a day* for his troops, and an equal amount for their horses, plus an additional 4–5 tons of straw per day for the animals. Such a horde would require 30,000 gallons of fresh water a day (hence their encampment along a river), and the removal of 2,000 tons of manure and 700,000 gallons of urine from animals and soldiers. Add to this the necessity for tents, firewood, etc., and the quantities and cost become colossal. Besides the necessary organisational genius, William had earned a reputation for paying his mercenary contingent well, including an allowance for generous amounts of ale, meat, fish, and wine to compensate for their delay. William had also made promises of generous rewards to his victorious supporters; he offered plunder and booty for the ordinary soldiers, and estates and titles for his knights and ranking nobles.

Reaching England in late September, William soon constructed a pair of defensive sites along the coast and began to branch out through the countryside seizing provisions, devastating the land, and luring English King Harold Godwinson into battle. Upon the death of Edward the Confessor in January 1066, Harold had claimed the crown – as previously cited – and spent the year as king defending the title against invading armies. In September 1066, Harold had successfully defeated a large Viking invasion force under the King of Norway, Harald Hardrada (who also claimed the Crown of England), near York in northern England. That decisive engagement ended the Viking threat and killed Hardrada.

King Harold Godwinson then led his victorious army to the south of England in order to meet the challenge of William. Following an exhausting forced march, Harold eschewed a delaying action and instead chose to stand and immediately give battle, occupying a strong defensive position atop Senlac Hill just north of Hastings on the English Channel. The outcome took a full day of brutal and grisly hand-to-hand combat of swords, axes, and spears to decide. The decision was in doubt until the approach of nightfall when, sensing victory, Harold's shield wall of foot soldiers broke ranks to overwhelm what they mistakenly believed to be the retreating Normans. Using their mounted knights to great advantage, the Normans penetrated and outflanked Harold's position, and slaughtered the broken English army. Harold and his two brothers, plus the cream of the English army, were scattered and cut to pieces in full retreat. The day, the crown, and the conquest of England all belonged to William.

William was to later build an abbey on the site of his great victory, Battle Abbey, near the small town appropriately named Battle. He led his triumphant army to London, sweeping any resistance out of the way, and on Christmas Eve of 1066 he was crowned King of England in Westminster Abbey. To his knights and nobles went vast tracts of land, estates, and rewards for their participation in the successful conquest. William at first attempted to engage and include receptive English nobles in his administration. However, in response to rebellious outbreaks of local resistance, he soon resorted to a program of harsh suppression. His relentlessly efficient scheme of destructive reprisals to rebels, and a violent scorched earth policy, mercilessly eliminated the former Anglo-Saxon aristocracy and fully implemented a political and social system of his own choosing and control.

By 1071 William felt confident enough to return to Normandy and oversee his Continental domain. By 1075, with the brutal crushing of several would-be revolts in Northumbria and East Anglia,

William and the Normans held England in a firm and permanent grip. His newly appointed lords and nobles literally fortified their positions by building an extensive network of castles throughout England. These castles served not only as defensive protection for their hosts, but also as a defiantly aggressive base to extend and dominate their respective regions. They became a symbol of Norman authority.

William's efficiency went beyond his military and political leadership; his commissioning of the Domesday Book to establish a survey of every English town, village, and hamlet was a formidable goal of enormous dimension for a medieval government. Due to William's keen eye for administrative management, he sought to discern the number of pigs, goats, sheep, etc., as well as who owned how much, and of what, throughout the land. It was a practical and useful tool for William's government and has become a rich source of historical information for modern scholars.

William's half-brother, Bishop Odo, a competent Conquest warrior in his own right, is generally given credit for the commissioning of the Bayeux Tapestry, a 250-foot-long linen and wool carpet elaborately embroidered to depict visually the various chronological events of the Norman Conquest. Beyond its historical significance, the sheer survival of the thousand-year-old piece of cloth is remarkable in the extreme. It remains on display to this day in Bayeux, France.

In 1053, William married Matilda, daughter of Baldwin V of Flanders and a descendant of Alfred the Great. For some obscure reason the marriage was not approved by the Church and the Pope until 1059. Perhaps it was due to William's illegitimate birth – his unmarried father Robert had no surviving heirs, other than William from his mistress Herleva – hence William's nickname of 'the Bastard'. William was always careful to correctly align with the High Church, and the invasion of 1066 was in fact conducted under the acceptance and flag of the Pope.

William seems to have been a faithful husband and the marriage to Matilda produced two future kings of England, William II (Rufus) and Henry I. Another son, Robert Curthose, became the next Duke of Normandy and a daughter, Adela, Countess of Blois, mothered Stephen, a later King of England.

In 1087, while campaigning in France, William suffered internal injuries from his horse bolting – he died shortly thereafter. He was buried in St Stephens Abbey, Caen, Normandy. The abbey was one of many that William had funded.

The far-reaching consequences of William's conquest and rule are numerous and significant. Feudalism, though already introduced, became firmly entrenched as Britain began to fully emerge from the early medieval period – socially, economically, and politically. Internationally, England was now politically connected to French Normandy and England's cross-channel relationships became increasingly active. England would now pivot less toward Nordic Scandinavia and more toward European France. The influence of French tastes in architecture, customs, culture, and language all became pervasive. The introduction of the French language by the nobility would begin the blending of the heavily Germanic 'old' English with the Latin-based French – the resulting language incorporating a wealth of words from each to generate a vivid and richly diverse hybrid tongue. Without question, the dramatic Norman Conquest of William the Conqueror in 1066 produced a seismic shift in English and world history.

WILLIAM II 'RUFUS'

Born:	1056
Died:	2 August 1100
Reigned:	1087–1100
Parents:	William I 'the Conqueror' and Matilda
Married:	Unmarried
Children:	None
House:	Norman
Illustration:	21. William II

William II, known as 'Rufus', succeeded his father as King of England in 1087. His older brother, Robert Curthose, inherited Normandy. The two brothers had frequently quarrelled and many nobles and barons of Norman France and England were therefore confused and anxious over the question of to whom they should owe their true feudal pledge of allegiance. There was some initial rebellion against Rufus, but it was soon crushed and the issue was resolved when Robert went on crusade to the Holy Land, leaving Rufus as regent over Normandy and King of England.

Like his father, Rufus was a fine soldier and a firm ruler, but unlike his father he had little respect for the Church and did not get along with its leaders. He was tardy in his appointments to High Church posts and used the vacancies to divert Church income into his own coffers. He had a long-running dispute with Anselm, the Archbishop of Canterbury, and Anselm eventually went into exile. Due to his ongoing refusal to get along with the Church, Rufus probably suffers in the medieval historical chronicles, which were mainly compiled by Church scholars and scribes.

Similar to his father, Rufus was a large, muscular man, with a ruddy complexion. He wielded ruthless control over his own realms, and went north into Scotland, killing King Malcom III (of Macbeth fame). He forced Scotland and Wales into compliant obedience.

Typical of the Norman aristocratic temperament, Rufus had a general scorn for most things English. Rufus led a hearty and extravagant lifestyle and was much beloved by his fellow Norman barons, with whom he shared both pleasures and gifts. He never married and was not known to have a mistress or to have fathered any children. He was known for a love of flamboyant fashion in his dress, and his court was considered to be scandalous in its behaviour. It has frequently been suggested that he was homosexual. His manner and personality in the eyes of the Church, both socially and religiously, did not win him any sympathetic portrayals by the chroniclers of his time or thereafter. For his part, Rufus was happy to ignore his would-be critics, who were prudent enough to keep their objections to themselves. Rufus's notorious temper was legendary and his pitiless punishments gave all serious pause for thought. As a vivid example, Count Guillaume of Eu, after being arrested for rebellious activity, was blinded and castrated while his cohorts were either hanged or mutilated.

In 1100 Rufus was shot with an arrow and killed while hunting in the New Forest of southern England. It was immediately ruled an accident and there was never a question of an uprising or rebellion in the aftermath. His younger brother Henry wasted no time in recognising his golden opportunity, first going to Winchester to seize the royal treasury, then quickly returning to London and a hasty coronation at Westminster Abbey. The guilty archer, Walter Tirel, returned to France without any consequence for his action which had been deemed purely accidental. There of course has always been lively conjecture as to the nature of this 'accident'. Henry, the Church, and nervous nobles have all been considered as agents behind Rufus's death, as well as the possibility that it was a combination of perpetrators, but no hard evidence has ever been produced. The transition to Henry was smooth and peaceful and Henry was well received. Certainly there was not a lot of remorse at Rufus's passing.

Rufus had named no heirs and had no children. He was buried at Winchester Cathedral.

HENRY I

Born:	1068
Died:	1 December 1135
Reigned:	1100–1135
Parents:	William I 'the Conqueror' and Matilda
Married:	(1.) Matilda (born Edith), daughter of Malcolm III, King of Scotland. (2.) Adela of Louvain
Children:	(1.) William, Duke of Normandy, and Matilda, Empress, as wife of Emperor Henrich V, and later wife of Geoffrey of Anjou. (2.) None. Over twenty illegitimate children from several mistresses, including Robert, Earl of Gloucester
House:	Norman
Illustration:	22. Henry I

Henry was the youngest of William the Conqueror's four sons. Henry's inheritance was without estates; Normandy went to Robert, and England to Rufus. Henry received cash, but was anxious to acquire land. Rufus's death while hunting in the New Forest provided that opportunity and Henry was quick to respond by seizing the Crown of England and eventually securing Normandy from Robert. Henry possessed a unique combination of cruelty, ambition, and judicious administration of his realm. His thirty-five years on the throne were ultimately marred by his failure to successfully prepare an acceptable line of succession, which would lead to a twenty-year period of political turmoil after his death.

William had groomed Henry for a possible career in the Church. He received a good education and became one of the few English kings up to this time who could read and write, and was the first of the Norman kings who could do so. His nickname was 'Beauclerc', meaning 'fine scholar'. Unlike his brother Rufus, Henry strove to embrace the Church and restore a warmer relationship with the ecclesiastical authorities. He recalled Anselm from exile and reinstated him as Archbishop of Canterbury, although Anselm later challenged Henry's authority and was again exiled. Better relations with the Church not only avoided conflict in the here and now, but would bode well for his treatment in the future chronicles as written by the scholarly clergy.

Most of Henry's thirty-five-year reign was marked by peace. However, soon after Henry assumed the Crown of England, his older brother Robert sought to invade England and add it to his own realm of Normandy. Through skilful negotiation, Henry outmanoeuvred him and thwarted this attempt. Later, Henry gathered the support of numerous Norman nobles dissatisfied with Robert's incompetent leadership, and in 1106 he reversed the direction of invasion thereby securing Normandy for himself. Upon winning the decisive Battle of Tinchebrai, Henry captured

Robert and imprisoned him in Cardiff Castle, where he remained until his death in 1134. By then Robert was into his eighties!

Henry was a skilful political and judicial administrator. He issued a Charter of Liberties to demonstrate his intention to steer a different course from that his of his deceased brother Rufus, who was viewed not only as scandalous in his court behaviour, but also heavy-handed and tactless in his governing. Modification of tax laws and legal codes were carried out by Roger, Bishop of Salisbury, whose efficiency in the handling of Henry's many administrative projects proved a marked contrast to Rufus's unpopular chief adviser Ranulf Flambard, whom Henry had dispatched to the Tower of London. Roger established what was evolving into a functioning civil service. The royal justice system was expanded and strengthened with accompanying penalties – frequently brutal and merciless – meted out to lawbreakers.

Henry's methods could often be cruel and violent. He had two of his granddaughters blinded in retaliation for the mistreatment of hostages by their father. In another notorious act, he had all of the 'moneyers' (coiners) at the royal mint mutilated for suspicion of debasing the coin of the realm – guilty or not. He later relented from such overt punishments by substituting heavy fines for lawbreakers, not so much out of compassion, but as a way to generate greater income for his treasury.

Henry was a prodigious procreator, producing at least twenty, and perhaps as many as thirty, illegitimate children from no less than six mistresses. Tragically, William, his only legitimate male heir and son of his first wife, Matilda, was drowned in 1120 at the sinking of the *White Ship* while crossing the English Channel. By then Matilda had died, so in 1121 Henry took a second wife as queen, Adela of Louvain, but no more male heirs were forthcoming. Henry then pronounced his daughter, confusingly also named Matilda, as his official heir. Henry forced his barons to accept this succession, but it was rejected after his death in favour of Henry's favourite nephew, Stephen of Blois. Henry could have selected Stephen, or one of his illegitimate sons, but instead chose his daughter, thereby plunging England into two decades of civil war, as neither faction could completely gain the upper hand politically or militarily.

In 1135 Henry died while in Normandy. He had a great fondness for the taste of lampreys, though he knew, and had been warned, that they were dangerous to his health. After consuming a large amount of lampreys, Henry was fatally stricken. He was returned to England and buried at Reading Abbey, an abbey that he had founded in 1121. The location of the tomb has since been lost.

STEPHEN

Born:	1096
Died:	25 October 1154
Reigned:	1135–1154
Parents:	Stephen, Count of Blois and Adela, daughter of William 'the Conqueror'
Married:	Matilda, daughter of Eustace II, Count of Bologne
Children:	Three sons: Eustace IV, Baldwin and William. Two daughters: Matilda and Marie
House:	Norman
Illustration:	23. Stephen

Stephen was the grandson of William 'the Conqueror' and a favourite nephew of King Henry I. He and the other high-ranking barons in England and Normandy had promised Henry that they would accept the succession of Henry's daughter Matilda as queen upon Henry's death. This situation had developed due to the death of Henry's son and heir, William, when the *White Ship* sank while crossing the English Channel. When Henry died in 1135, Stephen decided that he should be king and was backed by a large contingent of supporting nobles. This set in motion a period that some term 'the Anarchy', as the two factions surrounding Stephen and Matilda began an intermittent civil war that would engulf virtually the entire reign of Stephen.

In 1128, when Henry's daughter Matilda married Geoffrey of Anjou, many in England and Normandy feared a potential threat from France. Therefore, upon Henry's death there was much initial support for Stephen. These supporters included Roger of Salisbury, Henry's lead minister and adviser; the Archbishop of Canterbury, who was willing to crown Stephen; and even Matilda's half-brother Robert, the powerful Earl of Gloucester – although he later reverted to supporting Matilda in her bid for the crown.

Problems soon arose for Stephen: rebellions on the borders with Scotland and Wales, a rapidly depleted treasury, defections in the ranks of his baronial support, and the gathering strength of Matilda's forces. By 1139, Matilda and her half-brother Robert were in England with an army, and by 1141 Stephen had been captured and taken prisoner. Many were now acknowledging Matilda as queen, and although she secured the royal regalia, she was never crowned.

The struggle swung back and forth for several years. Twice Matilda narrowly escaped capture herself. Eventually her half-brother was captured by Stephen's forces, leading to a trade that released Stephen. Matilda's policies and personality eventually wore thin on her followers, especially in England, and her standing with the populace waned. In 1147, her half-brother died and the civil war had ebbed into a stalemate. By 1148, Matilda's military position and strength was in decline and she retreated to her stronghold in Normandy.

Matilda's cause was then revived by her oldest son, Henry, who raised an army and invaded England in 1149 and again in 1153. Stephen was now being supported by his oldest son and potential heir, Eustace, and the debacle seemed destined to go on interminably. Eustace, however, died in 1153, and Stephen, now ill, was growing more disenchanted with the endless struggle. Later in 1153, the two sides reached an agreement with the Treaty of Winchester, whereby Stephen would remain king, while Matilda's son Henry would be recognised as heir and future king. A year later in 1154, Stephen died and Henry became Henry II, King of England.

Stephen had many fine qualities: he was charming, popular, and possessed courage. But he was also weak in character, short on tenacity in overcoming a challenge, and lacking the political acumen essential for a medieval monarch. By the end of Stephen's reign, the dynastic struggle that he had precipitated had left him worn out, sick, and disillusioned. He was buried with his wife and son in Faversham Abbey, Kent, which he had founded in 1148.

MATILDA

Born:	1102
Died:	10 September 1167
Reigned:	1141 (but never crowned)
Parents:	Henry I and Matilda (Edith)
Married:	(1.) Henrich (Henry) V, Holy Roman Emperor, and (2.) Geoffrey of Anjou
Children:	(1.) None (2.) Henry II, King of England; Geoffrey and William
House:	Norman

We have a confusing surfeit of medieval English wives and queens named 'Matilda'. The one referred to in the above heading is Matilda, daughter of King Henry I. She is also known as 'Maud', the 'Empress', and 'Lady of the English'. King Henry I's eldest son and heir, William, died in a tragic ship disaster on the English Channel in 1120; Henry then declared his daughter, Matilda, heir to the throne. Upon this declaration, Henry required his earls and lords to pledge commitment to the succession. When Henry died in 1135, the nobles abandoned their pledge and aligned with Henry's favourite nephew, Stephen of Blois, whose mother was Adela, daughter of the Norman dynasty founder, William 'the Conqueror'. Both Matilda and Stephen of Blois had considerable followings and support for their claim. The result was a two-decade reign by Stephen that was fraught with rivalry, war, and uncertainty. The period is sometimes referred to as 'the Anarchy' due to the intermittent turmoil and instability.

A short identity list for the other significant characters named 'Matilda':

Matilda. Wife of William I 'the Conqueror'. Mother of William II (Rufus) and Henry I, both kings of England.

Matilda (formerly Edith). Wife of Henry I and mother of Matilda – Henry's declared heir to the throne.

Matilda (often referred to as 'Empress' and 'Maud'). Daughter of Henry I and heir to the throne as declared by Henry I. Mother of future English King Henry II (who, sorry to say, also has a daughter named Matilda!).

Matilda. Wife of King of England Stephen of Blois, and daughter of Eustace II, Count of Bologne. Stephen of Blois was Henry I's nephew and challenger to the throne of England upon Henry I's death. They too, unbelievably, had a daughter named Matilda.

Matilda, the lady who inherited the throne from her father Henry I, was a strong, determined, and forceful woman as befit her Norman heritage, but she struggled with diplomacy and was unable to form a coalition of barons powerful enough to maintain her reign as acknowledged monarch. Matilda did outlive her competition, Stephen of Blois, and saw her son achieve the throne as Henry II.

Married to the Holy Roman Emperor Henrich (Henry) V at the age of twelve and widowed without children by the age of twenty-three, Matilda then married Geoffrey of Anjou in 1128. By 1135, Matilda inherited the throne of England from her father Henry I, rallying early support in the civil war that ensued, and succeeding in capturing her opposing claimant for the throne, her cousin Stephen of Blois. Stephen was then swapped for Matilda's half-brother Robert, Duke of Gloucester and the illegitimate son of Henry I. Barons of each faction were nervous as to which side to align themselves with, fearing the consequences if they chose the wrong side. Matilda's husband, Geoffrey of Anjou, did not generate much positive appeal from either faction. Although Matilda's popularity steadily declined, her staying power and resolve never waned. In 1148, Matilda virtually abandoned the overt effort to claim the throne and retreated to Normandy, resulting in Stephen retaining the throne for the next six years before his death in 1154. Before Stephen's death, the Treaty of Winchester was agreed to in 1153, securing the succession for Matilda's son Henry, Duke of Normandy.

By 1154, Matilda's son Henry was twenty-one and ready to assume the throne as Henry II, the first Angevin (from the House of Anjou) monarch. Geoffrey of Anjou's nickname was 'Plantagenet' for the sprig of broom that he wore in his hat. This would become the dynastic name for England's royal monarchs for nearly the next 300 years.

Matilda remained in Normandy, strongly supporting her son Henry in various capacities, and dying near Rouen, France, in 1167. Buried in the Norman Abbey of Bec-Hellouin, her body was later transferred in 1847 and entombed in the Rouen Cathedral.

Her epitaph famously reads, 'Great by birth, greater by marriage, greatest in her offspring. Here lies the daughter, wife, and mother of Henry.'

HENRY II

Born: 5 March 1133
Died: 6 July 1189
Reigned: 1154–1189
Parents: Count Geoffrey V of Anjou and Matilda, daughter of Henry I of England
Married: Eleanor of Aquitaine
Children: Five sons – William, Henry (the 'Young King'), King Richard I, Geoffrey, King John I; and at least three illegitimate sons, including another Geoffrey and another William. Three legitimate daughters: Matilda, Joan, and Eleanor
House: Angevin/Plantagenet
Illustration: 24. The great seal of Henry II

The first of the Angevin dynasty, Henry II became King of England in 1154. In his time, Henry II controlled large swaths of Western Europe that included much of France, all of Britain, and parts of Ireland. Individually he was intelligent, energetic, and of course ruthless. He effectively used war, diplomacy, and inheritance to achieve both his political and imperial ambitions. He was married to one of the wealthiest and most dynamic women in medieval history, Eleanor of Aquitaine, and they produced two future kings of England. He had a great love of art and architecture, hunting, war, and law. His personality and accomplishments would dominate much of Western Europe during his reign and well into the future.

Henry reigned for thirty-five years and was responsible for the revision of English laws, courts, and procedures that would produce the basic idea of circuit courts, trial by jury, and the code of English common law. In 1166, the Assize of Clarendon established trial by jury as the legal norm. Significantly, the first legal textbook was produced and the tradition of trial by combat was increasingly phased out. The stamp of his remarkable personality was demonstrated in his imposition, insistence, and implementation of a rule of good order throughout his kingdom. This included curbing the powers of his nobility, forcing his barons to tear down or turn over more than seventy castles, and recovering offices and estates for the Crown. His reform and enforcement of law and order ranged from crimes of petty theft, to inheritance, to rights of widows, to property. He restored stability to England and Normandy after the troubled two decades of intermittent civil war between his predecessor King Stephen and Henry's mother, Matilda. In short, his impact on English, European, and medieval history was deep and extensive.

Henry was born in France, spoke French and Latin, and was basically a Frenchman. This would be true for the Angevins, and many of the later Plantagenets. From his father he inherited Anjou in central France. In 1152 he married Eleanor of Aquitaine, who was formerly married to the King of France, and in so doing he came into control of a huge and prosperous area of south-western France. But Henry also invested much time and energy in diligently ruling England. Though pruning back the independent authority of his nobles, he judiciously made a point of maintaining their loyalty and allegiance. This was to prove beneficial during the revolt of 1173–1174, when his now estranged wife Eleanor, in alliance with his power-hungry sons, rebelled against Henry. Henry was able to retain enough baronial support to suppress their rebellion. Eleanor was then imprisoned by Henry for the next fifteen years.

Henry was not only to quarrel with his ambitious sons, but also with his former closest friend and chief administrator, Thomas Beckett. Henry became entangled in several disputes with the Church and mistakenly believed that he could solve these problems by appointing his like-minded friend Beckett to the post of Archbishop of Canterbury. Instead, Beckett turned on Henry, reinforcing the Church's position to an even greater degree than before, much to Henry's dismay and infuriation. The upshot was Henry's famous rage, and the demand, 'Is there no one who will rid me of this turbulent priest?' Four of Henry's knights took him up on the request, travelled to Canterbury, and in the cathedral brutally hacked Beckett to death. Henry, of course, denied that it was his intention to slay the soon-to-be-sainted martyr. Canterbury rapidly became a prestigious and popular site of pilgrimage, with Henry one of the most public and vocal penitents. The murder of Beckett was to leave a stain on Henry's reputation, although many of the issues involving king and clergy were left for future generations to come to terms with – and violence would frequently be a hallmark of those confrontations.

Physically strong, bright, and possessed of boundless energy, Henry would eventually succumb to the fatigue and the frustration evoked by the relentless attempts of his sons to mount a rebellion and seize the throne for themselves. In 1182–1183, his oldest son and heir, William the 'Young King', led a failed rebellion. The young William then died in 1183, the second event being a sadder occasion for Henry than the first. In 1188, Henry's next-oldest son Richard allied himself with Phillip II of France, and when in 1189 his favourite son, John, joined the alliance, it shattered Henry's spirit and probably his will to live.

Henry II died in France at the age of fifty-six. Both Richard and John would go on to be kings of England. Eleanor, instigator of much of the sons' rebellion against their father, would be released from prison and go on to outlive all of their children except for King John I of England and their daughter Queen Eleanor of Castile. Eleanor of Aquitaine died in 1204 and was buried in Fontrevault Abbey, near Chinon, Anjou, France, beside her husband Henry and son Richard.

Henry's dazzling character and his lasting impact on Europe's future reveal him as one of England's most compelling and important monarchs.

25. Eleanor of Aquitaine, Henry II's queen.

RICHARD I 'LIONHEART'

Born:	8 September 1157
Died:	6 April 1199
Reigned:	1189–1199
Parents:	Henry II and Eleanor of Aquitaine
Married:	Berengaria of Navarre, daughter of King Sancho VI
Children:	An acknowledged illegitimate son
House:	Angevin/Plantagenet
Illustration:	26. Richard I

Richard the Lionheart was undoubtedly a great warrior of epic proportions. Blond, blue-eyed, and powerfully built, he became the personification of the chivalric warrior-knight. Richard was well educated, cultured, wrote poetry, and was decidedly vainglorious. He also was a Frenchman who, as king, spent less than six months in England. Richard spoke little or no English. He didn't particularly like England, and used it as a cash cow to fund his incessant warfare and pay for his exorbitant ransom; he famously vowed that he would 'sell London if [he] could only find a buyer'. He was fatally wounded by an arrow bolt to his shoulder while conducting a siege of a petty castle in France. The poorly treated wound developed gangrene, and Richard died several days later. His reputation has been celebrated in book and film, although the actual value of his reign was negligible. He has a magnificent equestrian statue in front of the Houses of Parliament, but contributed next to nothing in terms of concrete effect on English history, other than not leaving a son as an heir to the throne.

Richard developed his warrior skills at an early age and showed great prowess in conducting warfare. Early in his career he supported his father, Henry II, by effectively putting down rebellions, but Richard was soon at the front of his own rebellion against Henry in a bid to seize the crown for himself. Between 1173 and 1189, Richard pursued numerous alliances in attempts to overthrow his father. In league with his mother, Eleanor of Aquitaine, the estranged wife of Henry II, Richard eventually succeeded in forcing Henry to declare him his heir. Henry died shortly thereafter and Richard was crowned king at Westminster Abbey in 1189. Richard immediately left England and before the year was out had embarked on the Third Crusade in the Holy Land.

Richard spent nearly two years crusading and scored impressive victories over the brilliant Muslim commander Saladin. Richard's leadership and organisation of the invasion was well financed, efficiently planned, and skilfully executed – although it failed to achieve Richard's crusading goal of recapturing Jerusalem. Saladin did invite Richard into Jerusalem, but Richard felt himself unfit for such a sacred religious visit. Richard salvaged a partial success by signing a truce with Saladin that guaranteed Christian pilgrims access to all of the Christian holy sites in Jerusalem.

It was in 1192, on the journey home from the Holy Land, that Richard was captured in Vienna by Duke Leopold of Austria. Richard was turned over to the German Holy Roman Emperor Henry VI, and held for literally a king's ransom of 65,000 pounds of silver. This amount has been calculated as being between two and three times the total annual royal income of England at that time. Once again England was largely responsible for ponying up the cash, and Richard's mother Eleanor played a major role in obtaining this enormous sum. The amount was duly raised, the ransom paid, and Richard was released in 1194.

Richard married Berengaria of Navarre in 1191, while on his way to the Holy Land. They had no children and many speculate on the sexual preference of Richard. He did acknowledge an illegitimate son, Phillip of Cognac, but in some historical references there is an alluding to Richard's asking of forgiveness for sodomy, so it is often suggested that he was perhaps bisexual, if not homosexual.

Late in his career, in 1196–1198, Richard was responsible for the design and construction of the impressive fortress of Chateau Gaillard on the border between Normandy and Central France. A mighty enterprise, Richard incorporated the experience and methods of the great stone castles built in the Holy Land to erect this expensive and mammoth military structure to defend his Norman lands. His Norman estates were coming under more frequent threats from France, and Richard, enjoying his full-time preoccupation with warfare, remained on the Continent until his death, never returning to England after 1194. He temporarily halted the expansion of the French kingdom into Normandy, but between the reigns of Richard and his brother John, the great empire stitched together by their father Henry II was unravelling.

Much theatrical comment has always been focused on Richard's brother John, and John's attempt to take advantage financially and politically during Richard's absence on crusade. But Richard confidently felt that he could handle any threat to his crown from John, forgave him for any transgressions committed during his absence in the Holy Land and as a hostage-prisoner, and referred to John as a 'child'. On his deathbed, the dying Richard acknowledged John as heir to his titles and estates.

Richard holds an exciting and romantic place in the medieval world of knights, crusades, and chivalry, but his limited time spent in England, his endless and fatal pursuit of battlefield glory, and his disregard and disdain for the administration of England – other than to financially support his military exploits – supports the verdict of Richard as a failed king. Richard was buried in Fontrevault Abbey, near the tombs of his father and mother, Henry II and Eleanor of Aquitaine.

JOHN

Born:	24 December 1167
Died:	18 October 1216
Reigned:	1199–1216
Parents:	Henry II and Eleanor of Aquitaine
Married:	(1.) Isabella of Gloucester (later annulled) and (2.) Isabella of Angouleme
Children:	(2.) Five by Isabella of Angouleme, notably Henry III, Richard, Isabella, Eleanor and Joan. Probably a dozen or more illegitimate, including nine sons and three daughters
House:	Angevin/Plantagenet
Illustration:	27. John

John was the youngest son of Henry II. John and his older brother Richard rebelled against their father Henry, John being angry at his lack of inheritance – hence his nickname, 'Lackland'. Like Richard, John was encouraged and supported in this rebellion by his mother, Eleanor of Aquitaine, the estranged wife of Henry II. Henry later granted John an inheritance, the Duchy of Aquitaine, but this only further infuriated his rebellious brother Richard. John also lacked patience for obtaining whatever inheritance he might eventually receive. John was impulsive, impetuous, treacherous, and, as declared by much of history, incompetent.

Much of the criticism of John is justified: he lost Normandy and Anjou to Phillip of France; his nephew Prince Arthur was murdered, perhaps on his orders; he intrigued constantly against his father, brother, and many who had faith in him; and he taxed his lands to the hilt in order to unsuccessfully defend the Angevin family empire bequeathed to him by his father and brother. John was forced into signing the Magna Carta by his disgruntled nobles, and at his death, England was in civil war and under invasion from France. Not the most ringing list of endorsements to say the least.

However, John was never the complete disaster or the archetypically cruel tyrant he has so often been portrayed as. He had many strong qualities and probably achieved the best that could be expected under the extenuating circumstances into which he was thrust. Richard had already been struggling mightily to hold back Phillip and the French, and it was probably only a matter of time until the Angevin kings were driven from their untenable position on the Continent by the French monarchs.

Money was needed to fight these wars, whether it was Richard, John, or anyone else on the throne, and taxes were the means to that end. Richard had certainly cost England a fortune in revenue between his exorbitantly costly hostage ransom fee, his extravagant crusading efforts, and his expensive defence of the Angevin estates. John's criticism came as much from the negative outcome of his wars with France, as from the heavy taxation he imposed.

In 1215, the barons who forced John into signing the Magna Carta at Runnymede, near Windsor, were inaugurating a policy that would become England's distinguished hallmark for the future. This was the gradual reduction of absolute royal powers of the king and the resultant transfer to a group of co-governors, who were demanding a measure of approval (or rejection as the case may be) to the desires, acts, and policies of the monarch. This tension in the wielding and sharing of power between governor and the governed would be an ongoing struggle in the pattern of future *world* history. But it would make some of its greatest strides in England where the concepts of parliament, representative government, and participation of the untitled would grow, prosper, and eventually come to be accepted as the norm. It was John who would first endure the humility of this future.

The loss of Normandy and the Angevin continental European estates under John's watch forced England to concentrate more within itself, on language, culture, and defence. The resourcefulness of this island mentality would increase, even though the residual Continental influence would remain strong and enduring. Over the next four centuries England would repeatedly attempt to regain her foothold on the Continent, but in failing, would come to understand the strength and flexibility of being able to pick and choose her strategic participation in Continental affairs as the situation required.

Like numerous prior kings, John had bitter disagreements with the Church. His argument with the Archbishop of Canterbury, Stephen Langton, led to John's excommunication and an 'interdict' being placed on England by Pope Innocent III, from 1208 to 1213. Both of these edicts were later rescinded. Ironically, the Pope would later reverse his position and support John in his wars with France and John's intransigent nobles. In 1216, barons opposed to John invited Louis of France to invade England and seize the throne. The ensuing invasion resulted in a civil war that placed a frustrated John on the defensive throughout England and eventually led to his illness and death. While conducting a nomadic royal court, John suffered the ignominious loss of his royal treasure, including his crown. Misjudging the tide while crossing an area known as the Wash, his baggage train was swept away into an inlet of the North Sea, leaving John broken in both spirit and treasure. He never recovered. John's death, in 1216, ended the rebellion and encouraged the barons to reverse their policy and unite against France and evict Prince Louis from England.

John was twice married. The first marriage, to Isabella of Gloucester, bore no children and was later annulled. The second, to Isabella of Angouleme, produced five children, the most notable being King Henry III, who would succeed John at the young age of nine. Isabella would go on to marry the French Count of La Marche, Hugh de Lusignan, and produce another family. She was eventually interred in Fontrevault Abbey near the tombs of Henry II and Eleanor of Aquitaine. John was buried in Worcester Cathedral, as was his wish. John's son Henry was crowned in Gloucester Cathedral – London at that time being occupied by the forces of Prince Louis of France.

John's legacy is certainly curious. A spoiled childhood (he was Henry II's favourite son) certainly influenced the weaker aspects of his personality. He suffered serious setbacks politically, militarily, and personally, but he had many dedicated and loyal followers, such as the most able William Marshal, his chief administrator and regent for his young son, King Henry III. John had some success on the battlefield and generally receives high points for his organisation of the navy, restoration of a solvent silver coinage, and his personal administration of England – a kingdom that he took a particular interest in, unlike his brother and father who both concentrated on France. His direct descendants Edward I and III would become some of England's greatest kings, and in many ways he attempted to be a conscientious monarch. Though definitely not one of England's finest kings, he was not the totally cruel and incompetent failure his reputation so often portrays.

HENRY III

Born:	1 October 1207
Died:	16 November 1272
Reigned:	1216–1272
Parents:	King John and Isabella of Angouleme
Married:	Eleanor of Provence
Children:	At least nine, including six sons, of whom at least two survived, notably Edward I and Edmund Crouchback. Three daughters: Margaret, Beatrice, and Katherine
House:	Plantagenet
Illustration:	28. Henry III

The ongoing struggle between King John and his mutinous barons had two significant consequences that impacted his son Henry as he succeeded his deceased father in 1216. Magna Carta had been forced upon the reluctant John by his barons in order to limit what a king could do without approval of his nobles. Secondly, in response to John's resistance to their attempt to limit his power, the dissenting nobles invited Louis of France to assume the throne of England. Such was the situation when the young Henry became King of England. At only nine years of age, Henry was protected and supported by the loyal and most capable Earl of Pembroke, William Marshal. As Henry's regent, Marshal proceeded to not only help persuade the revolting barons to accept Henry as king, but also to reject, defeat, and expel Louis of France, while restoring good order in England. Henry III then embarked on one of the longest reigns of any English monarch, fifty-six years.

Henry III's reign was long and mixed. In a difficult and dangerous political environment, and under threat of French conquest, the nine-year-old Henry was first crowned at Gloucester Cathedral in 1216. Four years later, when conditions were more politically stable, he was formally and more lavishly crowned again at Westminster Abbey. Under the capable and loyal regency of William Marshal, Louis of France and his French forces were driven out of England. Later as king, however, Henry appointed numerous advisers from France, alienating much of his English realm. His French wife, Eleanor of Provence, brought with her a host of French relatives destined for high posts. His French brother-in-law, Simon de Montfort, Earl of Leicester, later led a temporarily successful revolt against Henry before being defeated and killed.

Henry aspired to be a strong-willed monarch, although in action and judgement he was frequently weak and ineffective. Henry enjoyed imported French tastes and culture, but to pay for expensive projects, such as the rebuilding of a grander Westminster Abbey, high and unpopular taxes had to be imposed. Expensive too was Henry's unsuccessful military attempt to regain Normandy, lost under his father John's reign. Henry's failed policies, high taxes and rejection of his barons' counsel placed him in similar circumstances to his father, John. Henry's continued rejection of the terms of Magna Carta and his unwillingness to abide by the Provisions of Oxford (1258) that further promised the king would respect counsel from his barons led to the Second Barons' War. Henry's military defeat in 1264, to Simon de Montfort at the Battle of Lewes, led to Henry's capture and imprisonment. De Montfort held both Henry and his eldest son Edward as prisoners, and as leader of the disgruntled barons, de Montfort acted as virtual king.

De Montfort instituted the radical formation of a Great Council, consisting of representatives from various shires and towns throughout England. This group of royal advisers would evolve into Parliament ('parler' being French for speaking), and become the 'speaking' place where these representatives would meet, speak, and advise the king – and even more importantly, also agree to raise money. The supremacy of de Montfort and the barons, however, was reversed in 1265, when Edward escaped, freed his father, and defeated and killed de Montfort at the Battle of Evesham. Edward was to extract severe revenge upon de Montfort's rebels, but the enforcement of Magna Carta's royal restrictions and the evolution of Parliament were now more securely in place.

By 1266, Henry had been completely returned to power, however, he took a less and less active role in government and politics – his son and heir, the future King Edward I, now assumed more of the official responsibilities. The Great Council would grow into a counselling body – the Parliament – and it was Henry's son, the future Edward I, that would gain notable battlefield success and achieve greater royal accomplishments.

Henry III died in 1272 and was buried at his newly rebuilt cathedral of Westminster Abbey. Henry, at his request, was placed in Edward the Confessor's old coffin, while Edward the Confessor received a magnificent new tomb, housed in a new shrine, which held pride of place for the newly canonised St Edward.

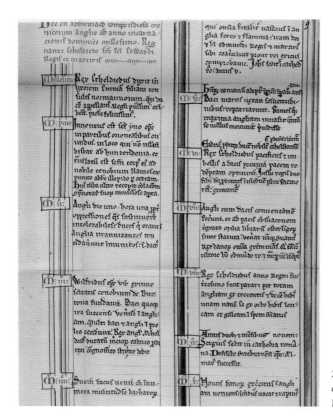

29. Matthew Paris described and portrayed many of the events of Henry III's life. A page from Matthew Paris's *Historia Anglorum* 1250-9.

EDWARD I

Born:	17 June 1239
Died:	7 July 1307
Reigned:	1272–1307
Parents:	Henry III and Eleanor of Provence
Married:	(1.) Eleanor, daughter of King Ferdinand III of Castile and (2.) Margaret, daughter of Philip III of France
Children:	Sixteen by (1.) Eleanor: four sons, notably Edward II, and twelve daughters, including Joan, Margaret, Elizabeth. Three by (2.) Margaret: two sons, notably Thomas, Earl of Norfolk and Edmund, Earl of Woodstock, and one daughter
House:	Plantagenet
Illustration:	30. Edward I

Edward I was a vigorous, dynamic, and forceful king. His energy, physical prowess, and military skill won him great success and respect on the battlefield. He was a pragmatic king who understood the value of Parliament, and that it could be used to his advantage to gain support and raise money. Edward was prominent in the administration of the evolving courts and justice system – in which he took a keen interest – and in establishing law and order throughout his kingdom. He was intent on curbing the power of the barons and the High Church authority, while reducing feudal rights and restrictions. He had a fierce temper and was ruthless in combat, but he could also be diplomatic in his conduct as a statesman. His background as a crusader in the Holy Land had given him great experience, and his exposure to the power and dominant influence of stone fortresses meant that Edward became a tireless builder of a large array of forbidding castles throughout the island of Britain. He was all that his father Henry III and son Edward II were not in terms of ability, leadership, and authority. More than just a ruler and a warrior, Edward was a leader with a legacy of social, cultural, and military achievements. He was probably the greatest of the Angevin/Plantagenet kings and a premier example of one of the most successful and effective medieval monarchs.

However, not all of Edward's efforts were benign, neither were they all viewed as welcome intervention. Some examples include Wales and Scotland, and the expulsion of the Jews from England. Edward's attempts at uniting all of Britain under one throne meant the conquest of Wales, the killing of the Welsh princes, and the elimination of Welsh independence by brute force. Wales was then brought under the English yoke and, in an attempt at reconciliation in 1301, Edward's eldest son was declared the Prince of Wales, a title borne by the heir to the British throne to this day. Edward's attempts at including Scotland in the fold of England's domain began with diplomatic endeavours, but having failed, escalated to the invasion and conquest of Scotland in 1296. There followed repeated incursions into Scotland to put down frequent rebellions, earning Edward the title 'Hammer of the Scots', a sobriquet that is etched on his tomb. These military adventures were expensive and in 1290, in order to help satisfy his need for funding, Edward saw fit to expel all of the Jews from England and to seize their wealth and property in the bargain. This situation remained in effect until 1656.

Edward succeeded his father Henry III in 1272 but had actually carried out many of the duties of king since much earlier in his father's long fifty-six-year reign. Edward had been captured, along with his father, during the defeat of the royal forces at the Battle of Lewes in 1264, by Simon de Montfort, leader of the rebellious barons in the Second Barons' War. But Edward extracted revenge upon de Montfort with a complete victory over the rebels and the killing of de Montfort at the Battle of Evesham in 1265. Edward then spent four years crusading in the Holy Land before returning to England. Many of Edward's powerful castles, strategically placed throughout Britain, bear a distinct similarity in construction and design to the mighty crusader castles of the Middle East.

Edward married Eleanor of Castile in 1254, and she was to bear Edward over a dozen children, including the newly crowned heir to the throne, Edward, Prince of Wales, who would go on to become King Edward II. Eleanor's death in 1290 was a bitter blow to Edward and he commemorated her death with a series of crosses erected throughout England to mark the passage of Eleanor's body on its journey for burial in Westminster Abbey. The well-known Charing Cross outside London's Charing Cross station is a copy of one of these famous markers. In 1299, at age sixty, Edward took a second wife. Margaret of France was only twenty years old and they produced at least three more children.

Tall and able to powerfully drape his long legs over a horse – hence his nickname 'Longshanks' – Edward cut an imposing physical figure. He looked, acted, and governed in a confident manner. His creation of a temporarily unified Britain, his reliance on and acceptance of Parliament as an operational extension of government, and his aggressive policies in administration of law, military command, and castle construction all project him as a most formidable monarch for the medieval era. Edward died in 1307 and was buried in an unadorned tomb at Westminster Abbey near his father and first wife.

Left: 31. An eighteenth-century depiction of the baptism of Edward I by Mather Brown.
Right: 32. The seal of Edward I.

EDWARD II

Born:	25 April 1284
Died:	21 September 1327
Reigned:	1307–1327
Parents:	Edward I and Eleanor of Castile
Married:	Isabella, daughter of King Philip IV of France
Children:	Two sons, notably Edward III and John; two daughters, Eleanor and Joan; at least one illegitimate son, Adam Fitzroy
House:	Plantagenet
Illustration:	33. The tombstone of Edward II

Edward II had large shoes to fill when he succeeded his father Edward I as king in 1307. Edward II, first and foremost, lacked good judgment. He was also a poor warrior, chose terrible friends, and exhibited behaviour that was strange at best and considered perverse by many. His accomplishments were few and his failures were numerous. His reign was inglorious and ended in his being deposed by his wife and her lover Roger Mortimer, in concert with a host of discontented barons. He was then imprisoned at Berkeley Castle and later murdered. His son, Edward III, would succeed him, and emulate his esteemed grandfather, Edward I, in success and reputation.

Edward II succeeded his father in 1307 and inherited not only the throne, but the chore of repressing Scottish rebellion. For this task Edward was to prove completely deficient. The Scottish leader, Robert the Bruce, had been a formidable opponent even for the redoubtable Edward I, and though possessing a smaller army, Robert had been gradually winning back Scottish territory through superior tactics and strategy. Matters reached a conclusion in 1314 when Edward's large army was soundly defeated at the Battle of Bannockburn. The inept Edward was humiliated in his defeat by Robert Bruce, and Scottish independence was now assured for three centuries. Not only were the border lands of northern England now exposed to frequent Scottish raids, but the decisiveness of Robert's victory completely exposed the weakness of Edward's leadership abilities. Disenchanted nobles now felt encouraged to challenge the weak king, who derived greater enjoyment from the pursuit of pleasure than assuming the requisite martial strength.

Edward's choice of friends and retainers had been questioned before he even became king. His closest companion, Piers Gaveston, had earlier been banished by Edward I, but Gaveston was soon recalled and granted a title by the new King Edward II upon his attaining the throne. Edward had been wed in 1308 to Isabella, daughter of Phillip IV of France and brother of France's future king, but while he was in France to gain Isabella, Edward appointed Gaveston as regent. To Edward's barons, the shallow and frivolous Gaveston was an insult and a travesty. Furthermore, much to the consternation of Isabella and Edward's nobles, Edward's personal behaviour and interests closely mirrored the contemptible Gaveston. Pressure from Edward's barons led to Gaveston's subsequent banishment and eventual murder, which only further alienated Edward from his wife and nobles.

Undaunted, ill-advised, and either unable or unwilling to learn from his past errors, Edward turned to two more favourites for his counsel, companionship, and affection: the Despensers, father and son. Both were deeply despised by barons and Isabella alike. As with Gaveston, Edward showered the Despensers with authority, privileges, and estates. The younger Hugh Despenser, like Gaveston, may or may not have been Edward's lover, but the question was and always has been posed. Certainly, the Despensers were lavished with extravagant gifts and attention, further infuriating the already heavily dissatisfied barons who now pursued a civil war with Edward. In 1322 the rebellious barons were defeated at the Battle of Boroughbridge, allowing Edward and the Despenser faction to wield power for the next several years. Fleeing to France with her young son, Isabella began an affair with Roger Mortimer, one of Edward's baronial opponents. Together they recruited an army, invaded England, rallied support among the majority of the deeply disgruntled nobles, gained approval of Parliament – thereby totally isolating Edward – and captured and killed the detested Despensers. Edward too was soon captured, deposed, and imprisoned in Berkeley Castle. Edward II's fourteen-year-old son was now declared King Edward III, and was later formally crowned following Edward II's murder.

Edward II's death in 1327 has been widely attributed to either suffocation, or more gruesomely, insertion of a red-hot poker up his posterior orifice. Either way, his disastrous reign was over, to be followed by the successful reign of his estimable and talented son. Edward II was buried in Gloucester Cathedral.

EDWARD III

Born:	13 November 1312
Died:	21 June 1377
Reigned:	1327–1377
Parents:	Edward II and Isabella of France
Married:	Philippa of Hainault
Children:	Eight sons; notably Edward the Black Prince (father of Richard II); Lionel, Duke of Clarence; John of Gaunt, Duke of Lancaster; Thomas of Woodstock; and Edmund of Langley. Five daughters
House:	Plantagenet
Illustration:	34. Edward III

Edward III was a chip off the old block from his grandfather, Edward I. He demonstrated many of the same qualities and attributes. He was energetic, enthusiastic, and determined both as a warrior and as an administrator. In England he was popular and successful. In his reign, English, as a language, began to replace Norman French as the 'official' language. Parliament was split into two 'houses': one for nobility and one for the representatives of non-noble birth from the various shires, towns, etc. From this entity, Parliament, Edward was able to obtain the funding for his larger projects, most notably his wars against Scotland and France.

Edward reasserted the English monarch's custom of claiming the title King of France, thus beginning the Hundred Years' War – a series of separated wars that would last for over a century. Under Edward, England gained the French port city of Calais in 1347, which she would hold for over the next 200 years. Edward also was victorious in 1346, at the famous Battle of Crecy in France, where English longbowmen defeated a larger army of heavily armoured French knights. Beyond some exciting battlefield victories and the capture of Calais, not many tangible benefits resulted from Edward's expensive wars with France.

In Scotland, Robert the Bruce had died in 1329, and was succeeded by his son, David II, but all did not go well for the independent Scotland, and Edward seized the opportunity to renew the Scottish wars. By far, however, the larger prize for Edward was France. Edward thought of France as his rightful kingdom, since his mother Isabella was both daughter and sister to kings of France. France of course rejected these claims. These wars were expensive, long-running, and inconclusive. By the end of Edward's long reign, they were being waged by Edward's martial sons, including Edward the Black Prince. Indeed, Edward's sons not only fought valiantly and successfully in Edward's name, but also remained loyal to him rather than rebelling or attempting a usurpation of the throne. Unfortunately for Edward and for England's political succession, the strongest son and heir, Edward the Black Prince, died before Edward, creating a vacuum of succession and leadership that would come to seriously plague England in the future.

Edward had succeeded to the throne in 1327, under odious circumstances. His father, Edward II, had been deposed, imprisoned, and murdered by an alliance between rebellious nobles, led by Roger Mortimer and Edward III's own mother, Isabella, who was Mortimer's lover-consort. By 1330, the eighteen-year-old Edward III was able to secure complete power for himself, capture Mortimer and Isabella, and establish his reign of England in full control of his own destiny. Mortimer was tried and executed along with other rebel barons who were deemed party to the murder of Edward II. Isabella was confined to permanent political retirement for her nearly thirty remaining years.

In 1328, Edward married Philippa of Hainault, producing eight sons, none of whom would become king. Philippa died in 1369, creating an opening for Edward's corrupt and ambitious mistress, Alice Perrers, to exercise power for a faction of nobles dedicated to her cause. By this time however, Parliament was strong enough in its authority to prevent Perrers and her followers from seizing power. Supposedly, Perrers was responsible for selfishly stripping Edward's body of his personal jewellery after his death.

During Edward's reign, the position of Justice of the Peace was instituted. So too was the famous Order of the Garter, one of chivalry's most prestigious honours. Increased international trade buoyed business, but also brought the Black Death, which began to strike England. By 1349, perhaps one-third of England's population had been struck down. This had severe effects on Edward's ability to wage war with France, but as was the case elsewhere in Europe, it helped end serfdom by driving up the demand for labour. Edward's eagerness and willingness to engage Parliament came from his need for money to wage his war against France. Parliament grew more essential as it not only became the collector of many taxes, but also began to determine where and when the money would be spent.

Near the end of his life, Edward grew increasingly senile and distant, a sad contrast from his earlier robust ability to manage his administration and his wars. He died in 1377, after a fifty-year-reign, and was buried in Westminster Abbey.

Left: 35. Edward III and St George kneeling at prayer.
Right: 36. The coronation of a king in the early fourteenth century, probably Edward III.

RICHARD II

Born:	6 January 1367
Died:	14 February 1400
Reigned:	1377–1399
Parents:	Edward the Black Prince and Joan of Kent
Married:	(1.) Anne of Bohemia, daughter of Emperor Charles IV and (2.) Isabella, daughter of King Charles VI of France
Children:	None
House:	Plantagenet
Illustration:	37. Richard II and his queen, Anne of Bohemia

Richard II offers a strange story. He sought an end to his grandfather Edward III's expensive war with France in order to save money, but had to quell the Peasants' Revolt over the issue of high taxes. He spent freely on a lavish and luxurious royal court, squandering any savings he might have gained through his policy of peace with France. His court was sophisticated and cultured, and Richard himself was a generous patron of the arts, sponsoring artists and authors such as Geoffrey Chaucer. He antagonised his nobles to the point of removing any hope of rallying an army to his position. He believed in being an 'absolute' king in the face of England's continued insistence on its monarchs adhering to limitations, as enforced by Magna Carta and the ever stronger and more robust lawmaking body, Parliament. Richard was abandoned by his nobles, forced to abdicate in favour of his cousin Henry Bolingbroke, and imprisoned. He was either murdered or allowed to starve to death while in captivity.

Richard II became a boy king in 1377, assuming the throne while still only nine years old. He had descended from two of England's greatest warriors: his grandfather Edward III and his father Edward the Black Prince. His father had died but a year before the king, thrusting Richard into the position of heir. On becoming king, Richard's main administrator was his uncle, the capable and respected John of Gaunt, the Duke of Lancaster. Early in his youthful reign, Richard's mentors were able to maintain a reasonable degree of calm stability and his future appeared promising.

At the young age of fourteen, Richard bravely rode out to Smithfield on the edge of London to meet with an enormous throng of would-be rebels demanding tax relief. While the rebel leader, Wat Tyler, was being killed, Richard soothed the masses with sympathetic pledges to look into their grievances and to be a champion for their plight. The revolt ended peaceably, although nothing was ever done in response to their requests and many of their leaders were later identified and killed. It was a most auspicious beginning for the young and seemingly courageous king.

But Richard, although not a warrior or war-maker, was also not a true peacemaker – he was an arrogant authoritarian who, due to the success of the Smithfield encounter and the diffusing of a desperate situation, was probably encouraged to mistakenly believe in his own false sense of power and ability as a sovereign. Richard soon surrounded himself with his own clique of frivolous favourites, reminiscent of Edward II's profound error in judgment concerning advisers. Richard foolishly alienated powerful nobles, who, with Parliament's backing, forcefully purged many of Richard's pals and reined in his behaviour. But Richard sought and achieved revenge with a ruthless vendetta against those who had stood against him. In 1397–1398, the Earl of Arundel was executed and the Duke of Gloucester murdered. Later, the Duke of Norfolk, Earl of Warwick, and Henry Bolingbroke (son of John of Gaunt, Duke of Lancaster) were all exiled. Richard happily seized all of John of Gaunt's estates upon his death, thus denying them to John's son, Henry Bolingbroke. At this point, Henry Bolingbroke decided to act. In 1399, Henry raised an army, rallied the support of other equally angry nobles, and, while Richard campaigned in Ireland, led a successful revolt to overthrow Richard and proclaim himself king. Now lacking any support, Richard had to submit and quickly abdicated in favour of Henry. Within six months, Henry was king and Richard was imprisoned, soon to die from either starvation or murder in early 1400.

Richard II had been blessed with intelligence, style, and fine taste in art and culture. His court was one of the most sophisticated in all of Europe. But he seriously erred in alienating the powerful galaxy of nobles that surrounded him. In particular, Richard would have been far better served by incorporating the likes of Henry of Bolingbroke into his realm of trusted councillors, rather than ostracising him through exile and provoking him to rebellion by seizing his inherited estates. The words 'Kill my father, but do not take my inheritance' were never more applicable.

By advocating a governing behaviour tilting ever closer to 'absolutism', Richard was bucking the English trend in which the power of monarchs was curtailed through tradition, written acts, and the growing strength of Parliament. Independent, selfish, and powerful, Richard's nobles were never going to tolerate a monarch seeking absolute power on title alone – without the commensurate benefits of a conquering warlord providing prizes, rewards, and glory. To keep these devilish nobles in check would demand a much stronger sword arm than Richard's. Although much of Europe was accepting absolutism, England was embarking on a different course. It was a watershed monarchy in the sense that it reminded English monarchs they would be limited in their royal prerogatives.

Only thirty-three when he died, Richard had already married twice, but produced no children. His first wife, Anne, died at the age of thirty-two without having given birth, and his second wife, Isabella, was only six when the politically convenient marriage was negotiated with the King of France.

To his credit, Richard had personally overseen the building of the magnificent hammer-beam ceiling in Westminster Hall, introduced the handkerchief, and sponsored the literary work of Chaucer. But as a king he was clearly a failure and his death was mourned by few. Originally buried at Kings Langley, Hertfordshire, in 1413 King Henry V had Richard honourably reinterred in a fine tomb at Westminster Abbey.

HENRY IV

Born:	4 April 1366
Died:	20 March 1413
Reigned:	1399–1413
Parents:	John of Gaunt and Blanche of Lancaster (John's cousin)
Married:	(1.) Mary de Bohun and (2.) Joan of Navarre, daughter of King Charles II
Children:	(1.) Four sons: notably Henry V, John, Thomas, Humphrey. Two daughters: Blanche and Philippa. (2.) None
House:	Lancaster
Illustration:	38. Henry IV from a stained-glass window

Henry of Bolingbroke, son of John of Gaunt and grandson of Edward III, received a good press from Shakespeare and had the benefit of replacing the failed Richard II. He was the first of the Lancastrian kings. He was a rugged warrior, a savvy politician, and the father of Henry V – one of England's great soldier kings. Coming on the heels of the autocratic Richard II, Henry provided a sharp contrast to Richard both in his manner of conducting a more austere court and in his more practical method of dealing with fellow nobles and Parliament. Henry was not above compromise and finding pragmatic solutions to resolve issues, but as a hardened soldier he was more than capable of excercising martial force to deal with rebellious uprisings.

Henry's claim to the throne was actually weaker than several of his other cousins, but when by mutual consent the time to oust Richard arrived, it was Henry who emerged as the leader and warrior who could command both armies and popular support. In essence, this is what kingly leadership is all about: being able to command, lead, and maintain a stable society. These traits are difficult for anyone from any social strata or station, but certainly being born to title alone does not guarantee this quality. This has always been the dilemma of inherited leadership – how to replace a worthless ruler when the incompetent monarch sits on the throne by birth.

Henry's rebellion removed Richard II, but his reign then had to withstand numerous threats to its own survival. As Shakespeare wrote, 'Uneasy lies the head that wears the crown.' The most serious of these threats were the decade-long Welsh rebellion of Owen Glendower and the rebellion of Henry Percy (and his son Harry 'Hotspur' Percy), Earl of Northumberland. Glendower's rebellion gradually merged and overlapped with that of Percy and another powerful noble, Edmund Mortimer, Earl of March. Several of these rebels, threats to Henry's reign, were killed or executed, including: Hotspur, Thomas Mowbray the Duke of Norfolk, and Richard Scrope the Archbishop of York. Henry rose to these challenges; through superior leadership, better military management, and sheer persistent determination. By the end of Henry's reign England enjoyed an environment of peace, unity, and loyalty that would bode well for his son, the future Henry V.

Henry was the first English king to take the oath of office in what we would call the 'English' language; previous English kings spoke and wrote in Norman French going back to William the Conqueror in 1066. Henry's son, Henry V, would be the first to write in 'English'. Henry IV and his wife, Mary de Bohun, produced six children. Mary died giving birth in 1394, and Henry proceeded to marry Joan of Navarre. His second marriage produced no children.

Henry had been predicted to die on crusade in Jerusalem, and that had been his long-held desire. According to the well-known story, Henry was visiting Westminster Abbey when he was struck by a fatal seizure. He was carried into an adjacent room and was told he was resting in the Jerusalem Chamber of the abbey. He died there, content to have died in 'Jerusalem'. Henry chose to be buried with his second wife, Joan, in Canterbury Cathedral near the shrine of Thomas Beckett. Both Henry and Joan are represented in lovely and well-preserved alabaster effigies.

39. The tombstones of Henry IV and his wife, Joan of Navarre.

HENRY V

Born:	16 September 1387
Died:	31 August 1422
Reigned:	1413–1422
Parents:	Henry IV and Mary de Bohun
Married:	Catherine of Valois, youngest daughter of King Charles VI of France
Children:	Henry VI
House:	Lancaster
Illustration:	40. Henry V

One of England's greatest legendary soldier kings, Henry V died at a young age, on the verge of possibly greater accomplishments. Instead, his infant son, Henry VI, became a reluctant and weak king, who would plunge England into the Wars of the Roses. Henry V succeeded his father Henry IV in 1413 and was the second Lancastrian king. He earnestly claimed the thrones of both England and France and married the daughter of the French king with an agreement to assume the crown of both monarchies. Henry was a true Englishman, speaking and writing in English. The English language began to be used in government documents and Henry V himself used English in his personal correspondence.

Contrary to the exciting Shakespearean tale of Henry as a gadabout who was late to maturity and martial accountability, Henry V probably had a pious, austere, and severe personality. His military responsibility began in his early teens and by the time he was sixteen he was already leading elements of an army at the Battle of Shrewsbury. At Shrewsbury, while engaging the Welsh rebel Owen Glendower and his allies the Percys of Northumberland, Henry was seriously wounded by an arrow to his face. Henry's vigorous defence of the realm for his father, Henry IV, was an ongoing commitment and there was very little time or energy for a dissolute lifestyle. His budding gifts for leadership, soldiering, and military planning were obvious at an early age, and with experience his talents only blossomed.

As a pragmatic politician, Henry attempted to unite England by welcoming its previously rebellious factions. He pardoned a potentially rebellious would-be claimant to the throne, Edmund Mortimer, who then became a loyal lieutenant of Henry, and he graciously moved the body of former King Richard II to a royal tomb in Westminster Abbey. His relations with Parliament were agreeable and he easily raised funds for his upcoming invasion of France. Probably Henry's greatest and most famous victory occurred at Agincourt in 1416 against the flower of French knighthood. Then, as at the Battle of Crecy in 1346, the devastating lethality of the English longbowmen prevailed against a larger and stronger French army of heavily armoured knights. Henry went on to conduct a brilliantly planned and coordinated conquest of France over both land and water. This campaign culminated in 1420, when French King Charles VI agreed to name Henry as regent and heir to the throne of France. Henry then married Charles's daughter to cement both the political agreement and the joining of the two royal houses together beneath one banner. It was an extraordinary coup.

Henry was more than just a brilliant and courageous soldier who excelled at inspiring and motivating his army, he was also a ruthless warrior. After his greatly outnumbered army had defeated the French at Agincourt, it became necessary to dispense with the difficult management of prisoners. Henry instructed his men to slaughter the prisoners and slit the throats of wounded French soldiers left on the battlefield.

Henry continued to campaign through France, an exhausting enterprise that led to his illness and death at the early age of thirty-five, with only an infant son as an heir. The prospect of Henry V's future for England is therefore left open to speculation. His body was returned to England and he was buried at Westminster Abbey. Henry's French widow, Catherine of Valois, would later marry Welshman Owen Tudor, and they would go on to spawn the Tudor dynasty of English kings and queens. Catherine would also die young, at the age of thirty-five, and be buried in Westminster Abbey.

Henry V's Anglo-French empire would be short-lived, but his impact upon English history as a purely English king would be deep.

41. The marriage of Henry V and Catherine of Valois.

37

HENRY VI

Born:	6 December 1421
Died:	21 May 1471
Reigned:	1422–1461, restored 1470–1471
Parents:	Henry V and Catherine of Valois
Married:	Margaret of Anjou
Children:	Edward, Prince of Wales
House:	Lancaster
Illustration:	42. Henry VI

A man who should never have been a king, and a man destined to fail as a king, Henry VI would be a pawn, removed as king several times, and eventually murdered in 1471 while still technically serving as king. Devout, pious, and well educated, Henry was never a warrior; he abhorred war and found happiness and satisfaction in the pursuit of learning. He actively pursued interests in music, art, architecture, and religion. Significantly, Henry founded Eton College and King's College, Cambridge. But politically and militarily, Henry was a disaster. Surrounding Henry were ambitious and conniving nobles anxious to take advantage of a monarch demonstrably feeble, weak, and completely ill-suited to his position. Not only was Henry politically incompetent as king, he also suffered from periods of severe mental breakdown, at times being completely out of touch with reality. His off-and-on fifty-year reign ushered in the Wars of the Roses, and resulted in the loss of almost all of Henry V's gains in France, not to mention a breakdown in royal succession that encouraged imperial murder, civil war, and violent political strife.

Henry VI was the only son of the great soldier king Henry V. Henry was not yet one year of age when he succeeded his father in 1422. He inherited a kingdom that was attempting to reconcile itself to governing newly acquired territory in France while paying for Henry V's wars and conquests. Even more challenging was the political juggling of numerous powerfully ambitious and independently minded lords and nobles who eagerly sought to grab for themselves the estates, titles, and lands to which they felt they were entitled. This entire burden fell on the shoulders of a one-year-old child. A tall order for any monarch, it was a virtual impossibility for an infant Henry VI and his co-governing regents.

Remarkably, Henry's regents managed to temporarily maintain this Anglo-French empire, even in the face of fresh French victories under their wunderkind female commander Joan of Arc. The eight-year-old Henry was crowned King of England in Westminster Abbey in 1429, and again in Paris in 1432 as King of France. But Henry VI was not interested in conquest, politics, or warfare, and the loss of France soon resulted. In 1445, Henry traded two French regions, Maine and Anjou, for the hand in marriage of Margaret of Anjou, niece of the French king, Charles VII, thereby infuriating many English nobles.

By 1453, Henry was mentally incapacitated and Richard, Duke of York, was appointed as regent. Henry and Margaret gave birth to a son, Edward, in 1453, thereby solidifying Henry's Lancastrian dynasty. However, with Henry unable and unwilling to recover political order, chaos, in the form of civil war, broke out. This was later to be labelled the Wars of the Roses – the red rose emblematic of the House of Lancaster and the white rose for the House of York. Both families virtually ignored Henry except to seize him as a symbol for their legitimacy to rule. The Yorkist faction captured Henry in 1460 and declared Richard, Duke of York, to be heir to the throne rather than Henry's son Edward, the Prince of Wales. This was short-lived, as Richard was killed at the Battle of Wakefield in 1460, and Henry was restored to Lancastrian control of the throne.

Through all of this turmoil, Henry played little or no role, and at times was not even aware of what was going on due to his mental illness. Richard of York's son, the capable Edward (by now Duke of York), declared himself king, defeated the Lancastrians at the horrifically brutal Battle of Towton, recaptured Henry in 1464, and placed him in the Tower of London. Edward then reigned as king from 1461–1470. Henry was now nothing more than a petty pawn, to be held as a token of authority by one faction or the other.

Complicating the plot was Richard Neville, Earl of Warwick, 'the Kingmaker'. He had earlier supported Edward, Duke of York, but in 1470 he returned to Henry's cause and once again restored Henry to the throne. Warwick, however, was soon defeated and killed by Edward IV (formerly Duke of York) at the Battle of Barnet in 1471. Edward IV again became king and set about disposing of as many Lancastrian nobles as possible. This included the killing in battle of Henry VI's only son, Edward, Prince of Wales. The year 1471 was triumphant for Edward IV (formerly Duke of York). He led the Yorkists to victory in several battles and was crowned King of England, having claimed the throne from 1461 to 1470; the previous heir, Edward, Prince of Wales, was killed; and finally, the pitiable Henry VI was murdered in the Tower of London. Confusingly, but convincingly, Edward was now king again. Henry was now deposed once more, and this time *permanently* removed by his murder in the Tower.

The tale of Henry VI is a sad one. He was a good person, but a pathetic king, doomed to endure his tragic fate by the mere happenstance of being born the son of King Henry V. He would have been successful and admired in many other capacities, but as a king he was miscast – and he and England suffered for it. Henry VI was buried at Windsor Castle. His son, Edward, Prince of Wales, was killed at the Battle of Tewkesbury and buried at Tewkesbury Abbey. Edward's wife, Anne Neville (daughter of Richard Neville, Earl of Warwick, or 'the Kingmaker'), went on to marry the Duke of Gloucester, Richard York, who later became the infamous King Richard III. Henry VI's wife, Margaret of Anjou, lived in France for another eleven years. She died in 1482 and was buried in Angers Cathedral, Angers, France. Her remains were scattered during the French Revolution.

The Bard, Shakespeare, could not have had a deeper and richer historical vein to mine.

EDWARD IV

Born:	28 April 1442
Died:	9 April 1483
Reigned:	1461–1470 and restored 1471–1483
Parents:	Richard, 3rd Duke of York, and Cecily, daughter of Ralph Neville, 1st Earl of Westmoreland
Married:	Elizabeth Woodville
Children:	Ten children: three sons, notably Edward V and Richard, Duke of York (the princes killed in the Tower of London), and seven daughters, notably Elizabeth, wife of Henry VII. Probably four other illegitimate children
House:	York
Illustration:	43. Edward IV as a child

Much of Edward IV's story was rendered in the review of Henry VI, with whom Edward played leapfrog for the Crown of England. Edward's rise to the throne came about due to the pathetic failure of Henry VI as a monarch. Edward's father, Richard, Duke of York, initiated the Wars of the Roses in an attempt to remove Henry from the throne and place himself as king.

There were many nobles who believed (and they can hardly be blamed for the idea) that the politically feeble Henry VI had to be removed. The civil war that followed eventually brought about the capture, removal, and death of Henry. In 1460, Richard, Duke of York, won the Battle of Northampton, captured Henry, and claimed the crown. Unfortunately for Richard, he was killed by his Lancastrian opponents at the Battle of Wakefield later that same year. Helping Richard, Duke of York, in his rebellion had been the powerful Richard Neville, Earl of Warwick (the Kingmaker), and Richard York's son Edward, who now inherited the title of Duke of York and the claim to Henry's throne. Edward was a fine soldier, excellent commander, and capable successor to his father.

In 1461, backed by 'the Kingmaker' Richard Neville, the eighteen-year-old Edward was crowned king in Westminster Abbey. Later that year Edward and his ally Neville destroyed a Lancastrian army at the brutal Battle of Towton. Having been previously captured in 1460, Henry VI was kept imprisoned, while Neville managed most of Edward's royal business. By 1464, Edward had decided to marry Elizabeth Woodville against Neville's wishes, as Edward now became more inclined to determine his own affairs. In 1470 Neville switched allegiance, and, in alliance with Henry VI's wife, Margaret of Anjou, and backed by the French, formed an army and invaded England. Edward IV fled and Neville proceeded to place the hapless Henry *back* on the throne – albeit with Neville still calling the shots.

This mad merry-go-round would be laughable it weren't for the lethal violence imposed by the various factions upon their brethren. These people meant serious business. When Edward IV returned to England in 1471 with an army of revenge, he quickly put paid to Neville's treachery. Edward defeated a Lancastrian army at the Battle of Barnet and Neville was killed. Next was victory at the Battle of Tewkesbury and the killing of Henry VI's son and heir, Edward, Prince of Wales. Finally came the recapture of Henry VI himself and his subsequent murder in the Tower of London. Still not satisfied, Edward IV had his untrustworthy brother George, Duke of Clarence, drowned in a tub of wine for an earlier betrayal.

The last dozen years of Edward's reign were stable and prosperous as order was restored to the political and social environment. Edward got along well with Parliament and (not surprisingly) the remaining Yorkist nobles. Edward shrewdly threatened an invasion of France, then withdrew his army upon a rich payment to return to England. His major error in judgment was designating his 'faithful' brother Richard, Duke of Gloucester, to be the protector of his children, including his young heir, the thirteen-year-old Edward, Prince of Wales. Upon Edward IV's death in 1483, the young Edward and his younger brother Richard, Duke of York, were both imprisoned in the Tower of London and mysteriously never heard from again – undoubtedly murdered. Responsibility has generally been assigned to Edward IV's brother Richard, who immediately claimed the crown, declared the sons of Edward IV illegitimate, placed them in the Tower, and probably had them both killed. The mystery has never been completely solved.

Edward IV died in 1483 and was buried in St George's Chapel, Windsor Castle. His daughter Elizabeth of York later married Henry Tudor, who subsequently became the first Tudor monarch, Henry VII. Henry Tudor's connection to the Lancasters and the throne was tenuous, but the marriage to Elizabeth and the reign of Henry VII spelled the end of the civil war period later called the Wars of the Roses.

44. Elizabeth Woodville, bride of Edward IV.

EDWARD V

Born:	2 November 1470
Died:	c. August/September 1483
Reigned:	1483, never crowned
Parents:	Edward IV and Elizabeth Woodville
Married:	None
Children:	None
House:	York
Illustration:	45. Edward V

The oldest son of Edward IV and his wife Elizabeth Woodville, Edward, Prince of Wales was only twelve years old when he succeeded his father as King Edward V. Edward IV had named his 'trusted' brother, Richard, Duke of Gloucester, to be his sons' protector. The young Edward had been living with his mother's brother Anthony Woodville, Earl Rivers, who had been in charge of educating him. Rivers was escorting the young Edward to London in April of 1483 when their party was intercepted by Edward V's uncle, Richard, at Stony Stratford, Buckinghamshire. It was a fateful occasion. Rivers was taken prisoner and later executed. The young, uncrowned Edward V was taken to the Tower of London, later joined by his younger brother Richard, Duke of York. Neither brother was ever heard from again, and it has always been presumed that they were murdered. By whom remains the question. Certainly Richard, Duke of Gloucester, who now became King Richard III, was and remains the most probable candidate.

Various dates are given for the two brothers' deaths, but sometime in the summer of 1483 is most likely. Their uncle Richard, Duke of Gloucester, had been busy. Besides capturing the boys and executing their Woodville escorts, Richard also arranged for Parliament to declare Edward IV's marriage to Elizabeth Woodville invalid, rendering the two Princes in the Tower illegitimate. This allowed Richard to proclaim himself heir and king.

Since most of the later history was written by the next dynasty, the Tudors, Richard III has become the most frequently accused of the murder, although he does have some defenders. There is a contingent of sceptics who believe the Tudors were responsible for the princes' deaths in order to place themselves on the throne. But there is little or no evidence for such a plot. Certainly Richard was responsible for his nephews' well-being, and in his care they disappeared. Richard also had a large motive – he seized the boys, then seized the crown. This remains the most commonly held explanation.

In 1674 the skeletons of two unidentified boys were unearthed in the Tower. King Charles II accepted that they were the princes and ordered their remains to be buried in Westminster Abbey. There is no proof that they are the princes, and until a DNA test is given to the bones, that determination too will remain in question.

RICHARD III

Born:	2 October 1452
Died:	22 August 1485
Reigned:	1483–1485
Parents:	Richard, Duke of York, and Cecily Neville
Married:	Anne Neville, daughter of Richard Neville, Earl of Warwick, 'the Kingmaker'
Children:	One son, Edward, Prince of Wales. Probably several other illegitimate; at least one son and one daughter
House:	York
Illustration:	46. Richard III

Richard III was the last king in the Plantagenet dynasty, a royal family that reached back as far as Matilda and her son Henry II in the middle of the twelfth century. Richard III has been portrayed for over 500 years as either the villain of villains and murderer of the Princes in the Tower, *or*, a competent king wrongly accused and maliciously demonised by those truly responsible for the death of the princes – the Tudor dynasty – and their great propagandist, William Shakespeare.

Richard III was the eighth and youngest child of Richard Plantagenet, Duke of York. It was Richard's father who pursued the Yorkist claim for the Crown of England against Henry VI in the early stages of the civil wars that were later labelled the Wars of the Roses. Richard III's father was killed in 1460 at the Battle of Wakefield, but the Yorkist cause eventually succeeded in placing a York, Edward IV, on the throne. Before becoming king, Edward had inherited the title Duke of York from his deceased father, and now his younger brother Richard became Duke of Gloucester. Richard was to prove a faithful and loyal ally of Edward IV and was rewarded accordingly with honours and responsibilities.

In 1472 Richard married Anne Neville, daughter of Richard Neville, Earl of Warwick, known as 'the Kingmaker'. They had a sickly son, another Edward (later Prince of Wales), but he died during Richard III's short reign as king. It was Warwick who had helped Edward IV achieve the throne, only to reverse his Yorkist allegiance and attempt to bring the Lancastrian family back to power. In so doing, Warwick was killed and Edward IV reigned supreme. Edward IV had two sons with his wife Elizabeth Woodville, including the future Edward V, who was being raised and educated by his wife's brother, Earl Rivers.

Edward IV died suddenly and unexpectedly, at age forty in 1483, leaving his twelve-year-old son as heir. Before his death, Edward IV named his trusted brother Richard as the protector of his young sons. This was a fateful error of judgment. Upon Edward IV's death, Richard proceeded to capture both of the young princes and place them in the Tower of London. Richard also saw fit to round up many of Elizabeth Woodville's family, including her brother Earl Rivers, and have them executed. Next he arranged for Parliament to declare the marriage of his brother Edward IV and his queen Elizabeth

Woodville to be invalid – thereby condemning the Princes in the Tower to be illegitimate and therefore ineligible for the throne. This then promoted Richard, Duke of Gloucester, to heir to the throne. Later in 1483, Richard was duly crowned king. The two Princes in the Tower were never heard from again and speculation was soon ripe that Richard III was responsible for their deaths.

Shakespeare, and other Tudor historians, have given Richard the image of a hunchbacked, gnome-like, deformed monster, obsessively cunning and cruel in his dealings with political opponents and deviously treacherous and unscrupulous. Richard was known as 'crouchback', but the irregularity to his physique was probably only a slight curvature of the spine, giving him a slightly stooped appearance. Richard's reprisals against family and political enemies, though not gentle, were no more demonic than those of his predecessors and contemporaries.

During Richard's short two-year reign, he is frequently cited by neutral observers in historical context for his able administration, patronage of the arts, and encouragement in the acceleration of trade; but there were almost immediate outbreaks of rebellion due to his self-promotion to the throne, his heavy-handed repression of the Woodville faction, and the widespread rumours of the imposed captivity of the Princes in the Tower. The Tudor upheaval did not come out of nowhere – there was already discontent with Richard as king.

Richard had already suppressed the Duke of Buckingham's rebellion in 1483, capturing and executing his former ally, while convincingly crushing the rebellion. But Henry Tudor's uprising of 1485 constituted an even larger threat. Henry Tudor, Earl of Richmond, along with his uncle Jasper Tudor, had fled to France in 1471 after the Lancastrian defeat at the Battle of Tewkesbury. They were now returning to England with an invading army and gaining momentum as they progressed through England.

Richard III was not a coward, and in August 1485, he bravely met and fought his rival at the Battle of Bosworth Field. Richard's army outnumbered Henry's, although a large contingent of Richard's army – 7,000 soldiers under former Yorkist ally Lord Stanley – held back, then switched sides to that of Henry Tudor. Richard III personally went down fighting, being killed in the melee and losing his

47. *Richard, Duke of Gloucester, and the Lady Anne* by Edwin Austin Abbey.

crown, which was later found hanging in a tree branch. The decisive battle placed Henry Tudor on the throne and ended the civil war referred to as the Wars of the Roses.

The body of Richard III was unceremoniously taken to nearby Leicester and given an impromptu burial at Grey Friars Abbey – the remains were believed to later have been flung into the river. In 2012, however, the body of Richard III was recovered from under the parking lot near the old Grey Friars Abbey area. Through DNA samples, the remains were compared with Richard's family descendants and positively identified to be those of Richard III.

The debate about Richard III and the true fate of the Princes in the Tower continues. The Richard III Society and other pro-Richard organisations have laboured mightily to rehabilitate Richard's reputation at the expense of the Tudors, and much positive truth on Richard has been brought to light. However, the weight of evidence against Richard remains heavy. He was given responsibility for the princes and it was he who captured and imprisoned them. It was Richard who seized the crown at the expense of the princes, and it was on Richard's watch that they disappeared and were presumably murdered. Finally, the successful rebellion against Richard did not happen in a vacuum; there was plenty of disenchantment with Richard's manner, authority, and methods. It took more than Tudor propaganda and the pen of Shakespeare to bring down Richard; there was already widespread outrage and discontent regarding Richard and his ruthless ambition during his reign. That is what led to Richard's undoing and the Tudor takeover, not the other way around.

Left: 48. Anne Neville, Richard III's queen.
Right: 49. The Princes in the Tower.

41

HENRY VII

Born:	28 January 1457
Died:	21 April 1509
Reigned:	1485–1509
Parents:	Edmund Tudor, Earl of Richmond and Margaret Beaufort, great-great-granddaughter of Edward III
Married:	Elizabeth of York, daughter of Edward IV
Children:	Four sons: notably Arthur, Prince of Wales; Henry VIII; and four daughters: notably Margaret and Mary
House:	Tudor
Illustration:	50. A cartoon depiction of Henry VII by Holbein

Henry Tudor was the last English monarch to take the crown by force of arms. It was Henry Tudor who restored peace and stability to England after the roughly fifty-year period of civil war which has become to us the Wars of the Roses. By 1485, many of the York and Lancaster candidates for the crown had been killed, either in battle, murdered, or executed. The crown had been seized and was worn by Richard III, formerly Duke of Gloucester and brother of King Edward IV, who had died in 1483. Edward IV's son, the twelve-year-old Edward V, had been under the protection of his uncle, Richard, Duke of Gloucester, but the ambitious Richard had captured and imprisoned the youthful monarch and – as most believe – murdered the child in order to secure the throne for himself. Resentful nobles, led by Henry Tudor, were determined to rid the throne of the ruthless Richard, and install Henry as king. Upon completion of this mission, Henry married the daughter of Edward IV, Elizabeth York, thereby uniting the houses of York and Lancaster. This brought an end to the tumultuous civil war period and restored order and amity to the kingdom.

Henry Tudor was born at Pembroke Castle in Wales. His mother, Margaret Beaufort, was a descendant of John of Gaunt – son of Edward III. Henry's father, Edmund Tudor, Earl of Richmond, was the son of Henry V's widow, Catherine of Valois. So Henry Tudor had a modicum of royal lineage, but it was tenuous at best. Henry's family had participated in the Wars of the Roses, supporting the Lancastrian cause, with his grandfather Owen Tudor being captured and beheaded after the Battle of Mortimer's Cross in 1461. Later, Henry, with his uncle Jasper Tudor, was forced to flee to Brittany after the Lancastrian defeat at the Battle of Tewkesbury in 1471. After the deaths of King Henry VI and his only son and heir, Henry Tudor became one of only a few viable Lancastrian claimants to the throne in opposition to the Yorks.

It was the York faction's willingness to destroy and devour their own family members through their own unscrupulous ambition that created the opportunity for Henry Tudor. Tudor, and other completely disenchanted members from both dissident groups, invaded England in 1485. Gathering momentum as their army marched through Wales and England, Henry's forces met those of Richard III at Bosworth Field in August of 1485. Fighting bravely and stubbornly, but abandoned by many of his prior allies, Richard III was defeated and killed, propelling Henry to the throne.

Henry set about binding the divided factions together and allowing England a chance to recover and prosper under a moderate administration. To demonstrate his unifying goal, Henry married Elizabeth of York, the daughter of the Yorkist king Edward IV. Henry shunned expensive foreign military enterprises while managing an efficient and frugal government. Several minor rebellions were crushed but Henry refrained from large-scale reprisals. He did see fit to invest in overseas exploration and commissioned John Cabot on a voyage that claimed land in the New World for England. His eldest son, Arthur, Prince of Wales (and not long to live), was married off to Spanish princess Catherine of Aragon; and his daughters Margaret and Mary were married off to the kings of Scotland and France respectively. All in all, Henry's rule was modest and prudent. His reign saw security and economic growth that would provide England and the next king, Henry VIII, with stable politics and a wealthy treasury.

Though he was not spectacular, Henry VII ruled for twenty-four remarkably successful years and died in 1509. He was buried in Westminster Abbey.

Left: 51. Elizabeth of York, wife of Henry VII.
Right: 52. Margaret Beaufort, Henry VII's mother.

42

HENRY VIII

Born:	28 June 1491
Died:	28 January 1547
Reigned:	1509–1547
Parents:	Henry VII and Elizabeth of York, daughter of Edward IV
Married:	(1.) Catherine of Aragon, daughter of King Ferdinand II of Spain (divorced 1533); (2.) Anne Boleyn, daughter of Thomas Boleyn (beheaded 1536); (3.) Jane Seymour, daughter of Sir John Seymour (died after childbirth 1537); (4.) Anne of Cleves, daughter of John, Duke of Cleves (annulled 1540); (5.) Catherine Howard, daughter of Lord Edmund Howard (beheaded 1542); (6.) Catherine Parr, daughter of Sir Thomas Parr
Children:	(1.) Henry, Prince of Wales (died age two months in 1512), and Mary I; (2.) Elizabeth I; (3.) Edward VI. Several illegitimate children, notably Henry Fitzroy, Duke of Richmond, by Elizabeth Blount
House:	Tudor
Illustration:	53. Henry VIII

One of the world's best-known characters, Henry VIII was a larger-than-life celebrity in his own time and has remained so ever since. His appetite for life was prodigious; so too were his desires for England and himself. His face and personality are recognised everywhere today, from gift-shop trinkets to large-volume biographies. Henry and his flamboyant story remain ubiquitous to even the most casual observer. Henry strode the Renaissance world as a giant personality of enormous contradictions. Physically handsome and athletic, brilliantly talented in many arts and skills, and possessing true visionary qualities in many of his manifold interests, Henry stood out as an imperial supernova of energy and egotism. He was also impatient, cruel, and reckless. He squandered the royal treasury on fruitless military campaigns, gorged himself on a gluttonous overindulgence in everything from food to wives, and conducted – especially at the end of his reign – a ruthless and tyrannical orgy of executions that has made the axe and the chop-block symbolic of the Tudor era. He is best known for two infamous achievements: having six wives and sowing the seeds for England's Protestant Reformation. Love him or despise him, his impact on English and world history is impossible to ignore and immeasurable in its ultimate repercussions.

Henry VIII was the second son of Henry VII. His older brother Arthur had been trained for kingship and in 1501, at the age of fifteen, had married Catherine of Aragon from Spain. Whether or not their marriage was ever consummated became a momentous legal question in later years. Arthur died in 1502, making Henry heir to the throne. Henry succeeded his father as king in 1509 and married his brother's widow that same year. In 1516 their marriage produced a daughter, Mary. She was to be their only surviving child.

From the start of Henry VIII's reign, at age seventeen, he was his own man – charting his own policy and making his own decisions. Henry consistently allowed his chief administrators to do the legwork on matters of policy, while he happily took the glory or credit for any achievements that were gained. Henry VIII revealed his true nature early in his reign when one of his first acts was to send to the Tower of London two of Henry VII's infamous tax collectors, Richard Empson and Edmund Dudley. Henry VIII was happy to gain public popularity at the expense of two loyal, if overzealous, civil servants, both of whom were later executed. At the same time, Henry VIII was more than delighted to reap the benefits of his father's efficient tax collection by freely spending from a rich royal treasury left behind for him. It was to be a common pattern for Henry VIII's reign: have someone do the labour, reap the benefits, blame the discredited underling for any negative results, and then have him, or her, executed. Henry VIII was a dangerous man to work under.

Left: 54. Jane Seymour, Henry's third wife and the mother of Edward VI.
Right: 55. Anne Boleyn, Elizabeth I's mother and the woman who caused Henry's break with the Catholic Church.

Henry's desire for a male heir was to provide the impetus for the two most convulsive features of his reign: his having six wives and the break from the Catholic Church of Rome. As Catherine of Aragon was unable to conceive again, Henry sought an annulment based upon the sinful marrying of his brother's wife. Henry's chief minister, Cardinal Thomas Wolsey, was given responsibility to solve the 'king's great matter'. Wolsey had been a substantial and effective administrator for Henry in foreign and domestic affairs, and had served Henry loyally and dutifully for nearly two decades. Wolsey had also enriched himself in power, prestige, and wealth, living and dining well and constructing a large, richly ornamented palace, Hampton Court Palace, near London. When Wolsey failed to obtain the necessary annulment or divorce, he was disgraced and fell from favour – all past accomplishments now ignored. Turning over his property to Henry, including Hampton Court Palace, was not enough, and Wolsey was dismissed. Wolsey would surely have been executed had he not died first in 1530.

Henry eventually bypassed the hurdle of the Pope and the Catholic Church with the clever and radical expedient of declaring himself head of the Church of England and granting himself a divorce. This allowed him to marry Anne Boleyn in 1533 and produce another heir, a daughter, Elizabeth. At the same time he was able to replenish his now depleted treasury with the lucrative policy of dissolving the wealthy Catholic monasteries. These monastic enterprises, containing vast possessions of property and land, were ripe for the plucking – which Henry proceeded to do. This policy was most ably carried out by Thomas Cromwell, who had not only helped secure Henry's marriage to Anne but also engineered her execution for failing to provide the male heir Henry so desperately sought. The windfall of profit from the sale of seized monastic lands and holdings not only enriched Henry's coffers, but also shattered a medieval way of life that went back centuries. It also extended the growing strength of the Protestant Reformation in England, a movement that Henry repeatedly disavowed.

Cromwell, following in Wolsey's footsteps, was adept at providing that which Henry desired. Even though Henry had been declared Defender of the Faith by Pope Leo in 1521 for his essay against Martin Luther and the Protestant Reformation (a title still held by British monarchs to this day), Henry willingly rejected Rome's Church leadership, and with this rejection came a *de facto* encouragement of the Reformation within England. Henry now felt himself not only politically supreme, but also the supreme head of God's English Church on earth. Not acknowledging this supremacy risked execution, as Thomas More, Henry's former friend and chancellor, learned in 1535 with his demise at the hands of the axeman.

Henry's next wife, Jane Seymour, brought Henry his male heir, the future Edward VI, in 1536, but his birth also resulted in Jane's death in childbirth. Cromwell's next choice for Henry's wife, Anne of Cleves, whom Henry vigorously rejected on first sight, helped lead to Cromwell's undoing and his trip to the scaffold in 1540. Henry's fifth wife, the young and vivacious Catherine Howard, entranced the now obese, sickly, worn-out Henry. His ulcerated legs with their stinking sores, and his bloated and repellent appearance did not excite the twenty-year-old. Her past and current infidelities were soon revealed, leaving a saddened Henry no choice but to send her and many of her household to the Tower for execution in 1542. Henry's sixth and final wife was Catherine Parr; more a nursemaid than a bedmate, she outlived Henry, who died in 1547.

During this continual search for a suitable wife and heir, the growth of Henry's state church, the Church of England, was laying the groundwork for a vigorous Protestant movement that would turn England from a stalwart Catholic kingdom into a Protestant-friendly nation. The ramifications would spill into the future foreign and domestic policies of succeeding monarchs, and would threaten England's national security through Spain's attempted invasion in 1588 with her mighty Armada. But

Henry had wisely, and heavily, invested in building a navy that would defend England against such an invasion threat. England's naval heritage would also generate her budding dominance of the high seas, which would further stimulate her expansion in global economic and military influence.

In fact, it was Henry's extravagantly expensive projection of English wealth and power onto the continent of Europe that, though failing to achieve military or territorial success, demonstrated to a Renaissance Europe that England was aggressively emerging from her medieval past. Henry gave England a national identity that proclaimed she was no longer a trivial island backwater, but a dynamic and outward-looking political entity possessed of military, artistic, and economic strength and importance. The robust vitality of this national identity would be personified in Henry's daughter, Queen Elizabeth I.

By the 1540s, Henry had degenerated into an exhausted and grossly obese old man, consumed by a variety of debilitating ailments. He died in January 1547 at Whitehall Palace, and was buried in St George's Chapel of Windsor Castle beside his third wife, Jane Seymour. Henry VIII was a massive man, with a massive personality. His faults and contradictions were in proportion to his strengths and impact – and that impact propelled England into a new era.

Top right: 56. Anne of Cleves, Henry's fourth wife.
Bottom right: 57. Catherine Howard, Henry's fifth wife.
Above: 58. Catherine Parr, Henry's sixth and final wife.

EDWARD VI

Born:	12 October 1537
Died:	6 July 1553
Reigned:	1547–1553
Parents:	Henry VIII and Jane Seymour
Married:	None
Children:	None
House:	Tudor
Illustration:	59. Edward VI

Edward VI provided Henry VIII with his one great desire – a male heir. Although bright and intelligent, Edward was born sickly and his reign was short-lived. Edward came to the throne in 1547 at the age of only nine years. During his minority he obviously required a protector, and after the religious and political infighting that had abounded near the end of Henry VIII's reign, it was clear that the child would become a pawn in the ongoing competition for power within the royal court.

Edward was born in 1537 at Hampton Court Palace, and was the son of Jane Seymour, Henry VIII's third wife. Jane, however, died less than two weeks after giving birth. Edward received instruction from a team of some of England's finest scholars and was given an intensive education in Greek, Latin and French. He was curious and loved learning, demonstrating a fascination with everything from military fortifications to international relations and geography. He was also raised a fervent Protestant and was well versed in the tenets of the Reformation that was sweeping through England and Europe.

Edward's religious conviction and ardent acceptance of the reformed Church would provide sanctuary and support for the growing Protestant movement in England. This became critical later, when, after his early death, his Catholic sister, Queen Mary I, doggedly attempted to reimpose the Roman Church upon England during her reign. Edward's brief reign of barely six years provided the foundation for the Protestant movement to fully take root and become entrenched enough to withstand Mary's stubborn attempt to re-establish Catholicism within England.

Henry VIII's sixth wife, Catherine Parr, provided Edward with considerable early care while he was growing up. After the death of his father, Henry VIII, his first protector was his uncle Edward Seymour. Later, after Seymour's fall from power, the position was held by the ambitious John Dudley, Earl of Warwick, who was later created Duke of Northumberland. All of these caretakers were Protestants and all reinforced Edward's Protestant inclination. It should also be noted that both Seymour and Dudley were later beheaded in separate executions due to their overreaching ambitions for political supremacy.

Edward VI never married, was frequently ill, and in 1553, at the age of only sixteen, died from tuberculosis. His death set in motion a short struggle for the crown that would soon lead to the reign of his older, Catholic, sister, Mary I. Edward VI died at Greenwich Palace and was buried in Westminster Abbey.

JANE GREY

Born: *c.* October 1537

Died: 12 February 1554

Reigned: 1553 (nine days), uncrowned

Parents: Henry Grey, Marquess of Dorset, later Duke of Suffolk, and Lady Frances Brandon, daughter of Henry VIII's sister, Mary

Married: Lord Guildford Dudley, son of John Dudley, Duke of Northumberland

Children: None

House: Tudor

Illustration: 60. Jane Grey, a depiction in stained glass

Jane Grey, the 'Nine Days' Queen', was the innocent victim of a devious plot by her father-in-law, the cunning and ambitious John Dudley, Duke of Northumberland, to place a Protestant on the throne following the death of Edward VI. Dudley's plan was twofold: keep the throne in the hands of a Protestant, rather than Mary Tudor, the Catholic and eldest daughter of Henry VIII, and continue to elevate the Dudley family's importance through the marriage of Dudley's son, Guildford, to Jane. It was a shrewd plan and might have succeeded if Mary had not rallied the populace to her cause, and if she had not benefited from a hastily raised army to back up her claim.

Jane Grey was born in 1537 and was not yet sixteen when she was proclaimed queen. Intelligent and attractive, Jane had been well educated in Greek, Latin, and Hebrew. She had lived in the household of Catherine Parr, Henry VIII's sixth wife, and her upbringing was deeply Protestant. Her mother, Frances Brandon, was the daughter of Henry VIII's sister, giving her a royal connection.

Dudley had manoeuvred himself into the position of protector and chief minister to the fifteen-year-old king. Dudley also realised that according to Henry VIII's will, Edward's half-sister Mary was next in line for the throne, and that Mary, as a staunch Catholic, would soon attempt to reimpose her rigid Catholicism on England at the expense of the Protestant cause. Dudley engineered the hasty marriage of his young son, Guildford, to Jane Grey; he then persuaded Edward to name Jane as his heir.

In July 1553, Edward died and Jane was proclaimed queen. Unfortunately for Jane and the Dudleys, the Parliament and the populace did not rally to Jane, but to Mary instead. With no army, and lacking any significant political and popular support, Dudley's plot collapsed and Mary became queen. A month later, John Dudley, Duke of Northumberland, was executed. Jane and Guildford were sentenced to death and sent to the Tower of London.

Hope of a pardon soon vanished. After Jane's father, the Duke of Suffolk, later became involved in Wyatt's failed rebellion against Mary, it was thought that it was too dangerous to allow Jane and Guildford to live. In February 1554, Jane, Guildford, and Jane's father all went to the Tower to be executed on the block. Her remains were buried beneath the small chapel on the Tower grounds of St Peter ad Vincula.

MARY I

Born:	18 February 1516
Died:	17 November 1558
Reigned:	1553–1558
Parents:	Henry VIII and Catherine of Aragon
Married:	Prince, later King, Philip II of Spain
Children:	None
House:	Tudor
Illustration:	61. Mary Tudor

Mary I, Henry VIII's daughter by his first wife, Catherine of Aragon, was born in 1516 and raised as a staunch Roman Catholic. Her gender and her religion were to have much to do with her future, her personality, her historic role, and her reputation. Had Mary been born a boy, she would have been a king and England would have been a Catholic nation, or at least would have remained Catholic for some time. Henry VIII's convulsive marriages and divorces may well never have happened, or at least not as frequently, and probably without their violent conclusions. Not only Mary's life, but much of history would have undoubtedly been radically different. But Mary *was* born a girl, and an ardent, daresay almost fanatical, Roman Catholic.

In early childhood Mary was doted on by her father, Henry, but that evolved into rejection as the long-sought male heir failed to arrive from Mary's mother, Catherine. Henry VIII's protracted divorce proceedings from Mary's mother, and subsequent declaration that Mary was illegitimate, was as depressing to Mary as it had been to her mother Catherine. Never completely healthy, Mary had always suffered from a variety of illnesses, some say as a result of the congenital syphilis that Henry had possibly passed down to her.

Mary was well educated in Greek, Latin, French, Spanish and music. Mary also took her Catholic faith seriously and practiced it with deep single-mindedness. After Anne Boleyn's fall from grace and subsequent execution, Mary returned to Henry's court. Mary seemed to get along well with her half-brother Edward and half-sister Elizabeth, and stepmother Catherine Parr, Henry's sixth wife. Mary adamantly refused even to consider conversion to the reformed Protestant faith, as Edward suggested upon his becoming king. Henry's will declared Mary second in line to the throne, assuming Edward was to produce no heirs, and upon Edward's death in 1553, Mary was declared queen.

After the failed attempt by the Duke of Northumberland to install the Protestant Lady Jane Grey to the throne, Mary was crowned queen in Westminster Abbey. Initially her assumption of the throne was met by popular acclaim, but that was soon turned sour by her marriage in 1554 to the future Spanish

King Philip II, and her virulent attempt to reinstall Catholicism upon England. Mary envisioned a Catholic heir to the throne and imagined herself at least twice to be pregnant with Philip's child. No child was forthcoming, and the pregnancies were probably false at best, and imaginary in truth.

Philip was technically King of England, although few references ever acknowledge this strange fact. Philip had no love for Mary or England and was happy to return home to Spain. His dedication to Catholicism was perhaps even stronger than Mary's, and he invested much time, energy, and a large fortune into the conquest and reconversion of the heretical England. Equally, England had no love whatsoever for Philip and the Spanish intrusion into their affairs. This fact would become plainly obvious in 1588, when Elizabethan England stood up to Philip's great Spanish Armada and destroyed it, to the utter frustration of Philip.

Mary's Spanish-based foreign policy also witnessed the loss of England's French port of Calais, the last vestige of England's territorial possession in France. This embarrassing loss could also be traced to Philip of Spain, as he had persuaded Mary to engage the French in an ill-conceived war that brought only sorrow to Mary and humiliation to England.

Mary's attempt to forcefully restore England to the true Catholic faith also met with stubborn English Protestant resistance, and only suceeded in earning her the nickname of 'Bloody Mary'. The more persecutions and executions that Mary conducted, the more determined her Protestant opponents became. Nearly 300 victims were burned at the stake, including Thomas Cranmer, the former Archbishop of Canterbury who served under both King Henry VIII and Edward VI. It seemed that her religious stubbornness was only encouraging her own unpopularity, and further cementing England's Protestant conversion.

A sickly Mary I died a sad and lonely death at St James's Palace in 1558 and was buried at Westminster Abbey.

Above left: 62. Catherine of Aragon, Henry VIII's first wife and Mary I's mother.
Above right: 63. The burning of John Hooper, one of Mary's first victims and the former Bishop of Gloucester.

46

ELIZABETH I

Born:	7 September 1533
Died:	24 March 1603
Reigned:	1558–1603
Parents:	Henry VIII and Anne Boleyn
Married:	None
Children:	None
House:	Tudor
Illustration:	64. Elizabeth I in old age

Elizabeth stands high as possibly England's most popular monarch; she combined the most attractive and desirable traits that a nation seeks in any leader, be they elected or by birth. Elizabeth inherited the forceful, energetic personality of her father, Henry VIII, without having the cruel ruthlessness of a despot. She possessed the practical and prudent survival instincts of Charles II, without his shallow, indolent, and dissolute lifestyle. She was a leader who, in a time of crisis, not only challenged her captains to succeed, but inspired them to do so, as had Henry V. She took religion seriously and understood its importance, without allowing its extremism to infect her domestic policy with vehemence, violence or retribution. Her age produced the flowering of a Renaissance culture of art and curiosity, as expressed through the tangible works of Shakespeare and the voyages of Drake. Though not without faults, Elizabeth's personality allowed her inestimable strengths to temper and overcome her obvious character flaws, and in so doing permitted her reign to succeed on a multitude of levels.

Elizabeth's career saw peaks and valleys that would defy the credibility of fiction. Born to Henry VIII's second wife, Anne Boleyn, Elizabeth was rejected by her father, first because of her gender, and later because of her mother's fall from favour. Henry finally placed her at the back of the inheritance line behind her younger half-brother Edward and older half-sister Mary. Edward's early death only increased the precariousness of her position, as Mary's intolerant Catholicism threatened Elizabeth's survival due to her Protestant leanings. But Elizabeth convinced her sister that she was not a threat to her reign, and lived to succeed her as queen.

There was great rejoicing in England upon Elizabeth's becoming queen after the rigid and narrow-minded reign of Mary. Within a year of becoming queen in 1558, Elizabeth had instigated the Act of Supremacy and Act of Uniformity, establishing her as Supreme Governor of the English Church, and completely restoring the practice of the Protestant faith – which would surely have had her sister Mary turning over in her grave. It also infuriated the devoutly Catholic King of Spain and former husband of the deceased Mary, Philip II, who had also entertained the idea of marrying the very eligible Elizabeth.

Elizabeth used her unmarried condition as a powerful lure in international relations, and as a coquettish tool to sway domestic politics. Elizabeth's flirtations kept everyone guessing as to her actual future marital course, both at home and abroad. She was wise enough to place great trust in her highly competent, loyal and dedicated set of administrators and advisors, most notably Sir William Cecil, Lord Burghley; his son Robert Cecil, Lord Salisbury; and Elizabeth's spymaster and devout Puritan spokesman, Sir Francis Walsingham.

Philip of Spain's retaliation to Elizabeth and England's religious heresy was his intended invasion and conquest of England by the 'invincible' Armada in 1588. Through a combination of fine seamanship, astute tactics and good fortune, the English Royal Navy scored a devastating victory against a numerically superior invasion force, driving the remnants of the shattered Armada back to Spain. It was the high point of Elizabeth's career, and ranks with Waterloo and the Battle of Britain as one of the turning points in not only the history of England, but also that of the world.

Elizabeth of course never married, and became celebrated as the 'virgin queen', the North American colony of Virginia being named for her. Probably her most enduring love was Robert Dudley, the Earl of Leicester, who, although married, remained dedicated to Elizabeth. He died in 1588, shortly after the defeat of the Armada.

Elizabeth's reign lasted forty-five years, and is often considered a golden age in English history. Elizabeth died in 1603 and was buried in Westminster Abbey. By the time of her passing, England had defied Philip's Spanish empire, embarked upon a colonial empire of her own in North America, and produced William Shakespeare, whom many consider the greatest man of letters in the English language.

Top right: 65. Francis, Duke of Alençon, who came closer than anyone to securing the hand of Elizabeth I in marriage.
Bottom right: 66. The seal of Elizabeth I, depicting the queen on horseback.
Far right: 67. Elizabeth I at prayer.

47

JAMES I

Born:	19 June 1566
Died:	27 March 1625
Reigned:	1603–1625
Parents:	Henry Stuart (Stewart), Lord Darnley, and Mary, Queen of Scots
Married:	Anne, daughter of King Frederick II of Denmark
Children:	Three sons, notably Henry, Prince of Wales, and Charles I. Five daughters, notably Elizabeth
House:	Stuart
Illustration:	68. James I

The first English king of the Stuart dynasty, James I of England was also James VI of Scotland. Both of James's parents, Mary, Queen of Scots, and Henry Stuart, were grandchildren of King Henry VII's daughter, Margaret Tudor. James was also a Protestant, and due to Queen Elizabeth's failure to marry and produce an heir, the crown fell to the nearest and closest Protestant relative. Conveniently, it also helped to heal the longstanding animosity between England and Scotland – a rift that would be gradually, but not entirely, healed with the introduction of a shared monarch.

James was already thirty-seven years old when he succeeded Elizabeth, and had been King of Scotland since he was one year old. He was a firm believer in the idea that kings ruled by divine right, a belief that would damage his relationship with Parliament and destroy his son Charles's reign.

James was known as the 'wisest fool in Christendom' due to his weighty comments on modest topics and frivolous thoughts on serious subjects. He was a mixed bag in features and in character. Intelligent, he wrote several books and famously commissioned the mammoth project of translating the Bible, producing the King James version, which became the standard English rendition for centuries. James was unattractive in appearance, uncouth in his mannerisms, and he slobbered and spluttered while speaking. His marriage to Anne of Denmark produced eight children, yet he preferred his relationships (possibly homosexual) with male favourites such as George Villiers, Duke of Buckingham; he showered the young Buckingham with many honours and titles.

James prudently retained Robert Cecil, Earl of Salisbury, as his chief minister and pursued a foreign policy of peace. Peace was also inexpensive, spending always being a concern for the more practical monarch. James's reign was relatively peaceful and tranquil, featuring the continued flourishing of the writings of William Shakespeare and John Donne. James was basically popular due to his unwillingness to tax heavily and his dislike of asking Parliament for more money. While James was on the throne, England established its first successful North American colony at Jamestown, Virginia, in 1607, and the Separatists (later called Pilgrims) and disgruntled Puritans began the colonisation of Massachusetts in

New England. James abhorred tobacco, the crop that was to bring wealth to Virginia, and felt that it was unhealthy, loathsome, and smelly – he was obviously a man ahead of his time.

James wisely refrained from entering the disastrous Thirty Years' War, perhaps out of frugality, yet he was unable to prevent it with his peace initiatives. He also encouraged Protestant Scots and English people to settle in the plantation of Ulster, Ireland – a policy that would have extreme repercussions for the future. James survived the infamous Gunpowder Plot that threatened to blow up king and Parliament in 1605. Guy Fawkes was caught as he was set to detonate twenty barrels of gunpowder in the cellars of the House of Lords. Fawkes, under torture, revealed the conspiracy and was executed along with several other conspirators. Guy Fawkes Night, on 5 November, is celebrated to this day with fireworks and bonfires.

James suffered a stroke in 1625 and died peacefully in bed. He was buried in Westminster Abbey.

69. James I, his son Henry, and his wife Anne of Denmark.

48

CHARLES I

Born:	19 November 1600
Died:	30 January 1649
Reigned:	1625–1649
Parents:	James I and Anne, daughter of King Frederick of Denmark
Married:	Henrietta Maria, daughter of Henry IV and sister of Louis XIII of France, kings of France
Children:	Four sons, notably Charles II and James II, and five daughters, including Henrietta and Mary
House:	Stuart
Illustration:	70. Charles I

Stubborn. If any word personifies the failed rule of Charles I it is that. He was completely stubborn and totally unwilling to find common ground and rule within the limitations that had become the pattern for English monarchs over the preceding centuries. Charles not only clung to the concept of the divine right of kings, but also to the autocratic concept of absolute rule. His cultured, refined and sophisticated court, coupled with his elegant taste in the arts, stood for nothing against his imprudent defiance of Parliament. He refused to acknowledge the fact that he was required to share the business of government, a tenet that had been evolving in England for several centuries. For Charles to defy this tenet of English government to the point of civil war would lead to his conviction and execution for high treason.

Charles succeeded to the throne in 1625 upon the death of his father, James I. A sickly child and a tiny man, Charles only inherited the crown because of the earlier death of his older, eighteen-year-old brother Henry in 1612. Charles's physical development was slow, but he progressed socially to a finer degree than his father. His court became respected for its sobriety, dignity, and appreciation for culture and the fine arts. Charles in particular had a fine eye for painting and patronised several notable artists such as Van Dyck and Rubens. But Charles began courting trouble when he married Henrietta Maria, the devoutly Catholic daughter of the French king. This troubled many Protestants in England, and her political meddling proved problematic during Charles's reign. Known as Queen Mary by many in England (a reference to the stridently Catholic Queen Mary I), Henrietta was also artistically inclined and favoured the elegant architectural forms of such masters as Inigo Jones. The North American colony of Maryland, originally settled as a Catholic refuge, is named in her honour.

Charles believed that he could rule without the necessity of Parliament. This proved difficult, since it was Parliament that provided the bulk of the royal funding for any expensive kingly enterprises such as war, new palaces, and maintenance of the king's considerable courtly retinue. Rather than deal with Parliament, Charles dismissed it for eleven years (1629–1640), and attempted to raise money through his own taxation method. This proved calamitous for two reasons: it failed to raise enough money to suit Charles's needs, and in abrogating his constitutional responsibility to Parliament he incurred the anger of many. Charles simply did not feel the necessity to negotiate, persuade, or compromise with Parliament, since he was convinced of his absolute power due to his divine right; in this philosophy he would not budge. Charles found himself short of cash to conduct a war to suppress a religious rebellion in Scotland, and was forced humbly to seek the money from a recalled Parliament. To Charles's thinking, resisting or rejecting the king's wishes was tantamount to treason, but he would soon see this accusation reversed and applied to him.

The confrontation culminated in the Civil War, between the Royalist forces supporting the king and those supporting Parliament (the Roundheads). Several pitched battles followed that saw early success for the Royalists, but under the dynamic leadership of Oliver Cromwell and Sir Thomas Fairfax, the Parliamentarians scored decisive victories at Marston Moor (1644) and Naseby (1645). Charles was captured in 1666 and kept prisoner on the Isle of Wight, all the while refusing to agree to any constitutional compromises that would limit or reduce his absolute power.

Charles was later discovered negotiating with the Scots, leading to a brief second civil war. The victory of Cromwell's highly trained and disciplined New Model Army at the Battle of Preston (1647) quickly ended it, but Parliament had had enough. Charles was taken to London, placed on trial for treason, and found guilty. He was executed in January 1649 outside the Banqueting House of Whitehall Palace. Ironically, the magnificent ceiling of the Banqueting House, painted by Rubens, had been commissioned by Charles himself. Charles was buried in St George's Chapel, Windsor Castle.

Charles's plea at his trial was 'no plea', claiming that a monarch must 'only answer to God', therefore ignoring his own earthly limitations, both personal and governmental. Not strong enough as a military leader to enforce his will *à la* medieval warrior, nor prudent enough to negotiate a political solution across the bargaining table, Charles succumbed to his delusions of authoritarian grandeur. He decided he would martyr himself to prove the righteousness of his belief in absolute divine right of power. He was correct in the sense that he died a martyr's death with dignified courage, but was dead wrong, literally, in the cause that he championed. Charles worked against his own best interests, because he selfishly refused to accept the voice of those whose interests he was charged to lead – his subjects.

71. Henrietta Maria, by Sir Anthony van Dyck.

49

OLIVER CROMWELL

Born:	25 April 1599
Died:	3 September 1658
Interregnum:	1649–1658 (His son Richard Cromwell: 1658–1659)
Parents:	Robert Cromwell and Elizabeth Stewart
Married:	Elizabeth Bourchier
Children:	Five sons: Richard, Robert, Oliver, Henry, and James. Four daughters: Elizabeth Frances, Mary, and Bridget
Illustration:	72. Oliver Cromwell

England's first and only experiment with being a republic took place after the trial and execution of King Charles I in 1649. Leading the effort was a gentleman and Member of Parliament, Oliver Cromwell. Cromwell was also a devout Puritan who opposed Charles I's methods, attitude, and obstinacy. Charles had not only chosen to rule as an absolute monarch with the right of divine powers, but had dismissed any obligation or association with England's representative governing body – Parliament. This was less a problem for Charles until he required money to finance his wars. Charles's clumsy and heavy-handed attempts to ignore, dictate to, and later arrest those in Parliament who opposed him brought on a civil war that would end in Charles's defeat, trial and execution. Oliver Cromwell would organise and lead the army that would defeat Charles's Royalist forces on the battlefield. He would force Charles to surrender and submit to governing within Parliament's boundaries, and when he refused to cooperate, place him on trial and demand his execution for treason.

Cromwell had not been trained as a soldier, but discovered a natural talent as a military leader, organiser, and tactician. His early success as a leader of cavalry, followed by his request to Parliament to establish a New Model Army, demonstrated his consummate skill as a professional soldier. Parliament's New Model Army under Cromwell's skilled direction won decisive victories over Charles's Royalist forces at the battles of Marston Moor (1644), Naseby (1645), and later over Charles's son and heir at Worcester (1651). After Charles's execution, Parliament declared a Commonwealth to be operated under a loose form of republican management. When this proved unwieldy, Cromwell emerged as leader with the title of Lord Protector. Cromwell was offered the crown, which would have taken the uprising full circle, but he declined.

Parliament operated as the Commonwealth from 1649 to 1653 and under the Protectorate from 1653 to 1659. This decade was marked by several wars, strict Puritan social controls, and a general drifting of governmental direction as England sought to identify how it would be governed. Cromwell led armies that carried out the ruthless quashing of rebellions in Ireland and Scotland; these wars involved religion as much as politics. Cromwell's role in the suppression of the Irish Rebellion has been greatly debated and still is subject to much conjecture. Later international conflicts involved wars with the Dutch and with Spain.

Cromwell died in 1658, and was replaced by his son Richard Cromwell. Richard, however, had little support, experience, or interest in either military or political leadership, and shortly resigned his post as Lord Protector. One of Parliament's leading generals, George Monck, brought a well-commanded army into London and arranged for Parliament to invite Charles II to return to England to assume the throne – which he proceeded to do. England's great experiment with being a republic had ended. However, monarchs would now rule with Parliament's favour and permission, rather than the other way round.

Oliver Cromwell was buried in Westminster Abbey, only to be disinterred by Charles II in 1691, then hanged, drawn and quartered, and his head placed on a pole outside Westminster Hall for the next decade. A fine statue of Oliver Cromwell now stands outside Parliament's Palace of Westminster. Richard Cromwell retreated into relative obscurity after resigning his post. He travelled throughout Europe for the next two decades, returned to England, and lived out his life peacefully, dying in 1712 at the age of eighty-five.

73. Oliver Cromwell.

50

CHARLES II

Born:	29 May 1630
Died:	6 February 1685
Reigned:	1660–1685
Parents:	Charles I and Henrietta Maria
Married:	Catherine of Braganza, daughter of the King of Portugal
Children:	None from his wife. At least thirteen illegitimate children, notably James Scott, Duke of Monmouth
House:	Stuart
Illustration:	74. Charles II

Charles II, the 'merry monarch' who was restored to the throne in 1660 after nearly a dozen years of strict rule by Oliver Cromwell and the Puritan Parliament (the Interregnum), provided a breath of fresh air for England's population. Under Charles's reign a glittering court life returned and thrived, theatres and taverns reopened, and openly festive displays for religious celebrations, such as Christmas, began again to be enjoyed. Charles himself practised a dissolute lifestyle with such joyous abandon that his behaviour would have been shunned not only by the intolerant Puritans, but also by his morally self-righteous father, Charles I.

Charles II was charming, flexible, and tolerant, seeking to live and let live as long as he and his subjects remained within the political and religious boundaries necessary for his prosperous survival. Unlike his stubborn and rigid father Charles I, Charles II was first and foremost a survivor; within his clever and witty personality there was a willingness to bend and reshape himself to whatever policy was necessary to forward and maintain his position. Charles radiated the happy desire to enjoy life and to have a good time. Both in exile and as king, he was careful to avoid placing himself in an untenable political position that would endanger his well-being.

Not that he was a coward, quite the contrary. Charles had fought bravely with his father against the Parliamentarians in the Civil War, before fleeing to France in 1645. After Charles I's execution in 1649, Charles II returned to England to claim the crown, only to be decisively defeated in 1651 at the Battle of Worcester. It was after this engagement that Charles famously hid in an oak tree to avoid capture by Cromwell's soldiers. For the rest of his life Charles loved to regale an audience with this tale. Later, Charles again escaped to the Continent, where he remained in exile over the next decade, biding his time until Cromwell's death and the gradual decay of the Parliamentarian government. His patience and persistence were rewarded in 1660 when he was invited to return to England and assume the throne.

Charles led a flamboyantly ribald life saturated with wine and mistresses. He produced over a dozen illegitimate children (although no legitimate ones from his wife) from numerous relationships with such well-known mistresses as Nell Gwynn, Lucy Walter, and Barbra Villiers. To pay for his extravagant court life Charles was willing to get along with Parliament, although Parliament was always suspicious that Charles was a closet Catholic (which he was), and that he harboured a deeper acceptance for his father's absolute monarchist views. Charles was prudent enough to keep any such opinions well hidden. In 1660, upon Charles's return to England, Parliament paid for new coronation regalia to replace those which had previously been destroyed during the Interregnum. These remain as the crown jewels that are still used and displayed to this day.

Besides his lusty, amoral and amiable behaviour, Charles was a promoter and patron of science and the arts. The Royal Society, the Royal Observatory, and the Royal Hospital at Chelsea for army pensioners, which Charles supposedly founded on the insistence of his mistress Nell Gwynn, were all sponsored by the king. Charles was the personal patron of the architect Sir Christopher Wren, responsible for the rebuilding of St Paul's Cathedral after the disastrous Great Fire of London in 1666. The Great Fire destroyed virtually all of London and came on the heels of the Great Plague of 1665. The tragic Great Fire had several major benefits, however, as it allowed a new London to be rebuilt and wiped out acres of rat-infested areas, which had spawned the previous year's plague.

Charles suffered a stroke in 1685 and never recovered. On his deathbed he openly converted and took the last rites as a Roman Catholic. For several years Charles had been secretly receiving payments from France on a promise to reintroduce Roman Catholicism into England – a promise he probably never intended to keep, and another example of his penchant for playing on all sides of the table in order to promote and protect his own position. Ironically, he was buried in an Anglican service at Westminster Abbey. Such was Charles II.

75. The restoration of Charles II at Cheapside, by William Hogarth.

51

JAMES II

Born:	14 October 1633
Died:	6 September 1701
Reigned:	1685–1688/1689
Parents:	Charles I and Henrietta Maria
Married:	(1.) Anne Hyde and (2.) Mary of Modena
Children:	(1.) Four sons and four daughters, notably Mary II and Anne. (2.) Two sons, notably James ('The Old Pretender'), and five daughters. At least five illegitimate children
House:	Stuart
Illustration:	76. Detail from a picture showing the coronation of James II in Westminster Abbey

As an administrator, military commander, and public servant, James Stuart, Duke of York, was competent and professional. When his brother, King Charles II, failed to produce a legitimate heir to the throne, James became the heir apparent, succeeding Charles in 1685. Whereas Charles was affable, moderate, and willing to compromise in order to insure his political survival, James was humourless, strident, and heavy-handed in his approach to governing. While Charles tempered his religious position and waited until he was dying to convert to Catholicism, James openly and foolishly flaunted his Catholic religion. James made no secret of his attempt to impose his political and religious convictions, and there were many who feared that James was beginning a policy to resurrect Charles I's rule by absolute authority, and to reimpose Roman Catholicism on England. The result was a short and unpopular reign; James was peacefully removed in 1688, during what became known as the Glorious Revolution.

James was the younger son of Charles I and fled to the Continent on the arrest and execution of his father. While in Europe he served as a brave and effective commander in both the French and Spanish armies. James returned to England upon the restoration of his brother Charles II to the throne (1660), and was placed in charge of the Royal Navy as Lord High Admiral. Once again he performed efficiently and effectively, leading the fleet to victory over the Dutch at the Battle of Lowestoft (1665) and again at Sole Bay (1672). When England seized the Dutch North American colony of New Netherlands, it was the Royal Navy that provided the punch that achieved the conquest. New Netherlands was renamed New York, and the colonial capital of New Amsterdam became New York City, in tribute to James Stuart, Duke of York.

It was at this time that James, against the advice of his brother Charles II, converted to Catholicism and resigned his post as Lord High Admiral. The religious question was still a highly volatile issue, and England's position, both in Parliament and in public consensus, was to avoid at all costs the potential for the outbreak of a religious war. Therefore, though Catholics were tolerated, Protestants maintained most royal and governmental positions. This policy was reinforced by the Test Act of 1673, which demanded that all holders of public office swear anti-Catholic, pro-Anglican Church allegiance. In response to James's conversion, the ever-alert and politically agile Charles ordered James's daughters to be raised as Protestants.

James's marriage to Anne Hyde in 1660 produced two surviving adult daughters, Mary and Anne – both future queens. He also sired at least five illegitimate children by his mistresses. Problems developed later after Anne Hyde died in 1671, and James chose a fifteen-year-old Italian princess, Mary of Modena, to be his Catholic bride in 1673. Later, when a Catholic son was born, it was to have serious consequences for the future succession.

It was not long after James succeeded Charles as king in 1685 that James's pro-Catholic, arrogant, high-handed policies incited rebellion. The first attempt to overthrow James came from Charles II's illegitimate Protestant son, James Scott, Duke of Monmouth. It was poorly conducted and supported, and was ruthlessly crushed at the Battle of Sedgemoor in 1685. Monmouth was captured and executed along with many of his followers in a vicious roundup of rebels known as the Bloody Assizes. James II's problems only increased with the birth of his son in 1688 and the looming threat of a Catholic heir to the throne. These policies were to override many of James's positive attributes.

James had shown many fine qualities of leadership earlier in his career; militarily and domestically. During the Great Fire of London in 1666, the future King James II had taken charge of firefighting and his actions were greatly praised and admired. His loyalty, bravery and energy were never questioned, but unfortunately, his arrogance, stubbornness and lack of good judgment in the political environment provoked widespread distrust and fear, and therefore led to his failure as a monarch.

Late in 1688, William of Orange, a devout Protestant from Holland and husband of Mary (James II's Protestant daughter), invaded England and was warmly received. James II's army quickly abandoned James and went over to William, encouraging James to flee to France. Parliament quickly invited William and Mary to accept the throne, which they did.

James II later returned with an invasion force of his own, but was decisively defeated in Ireland at the Battle of the Boyne in 1690. James returned to France and lived in exile, dying in 1701. His body was buried in France at St Germain-en-Laye, but later moved to the church of the English Benedictines in Paris. His son James and grandson Charles (Bonny Prince Charlie) both attempted invasions of England in order to reclaim the crown. Both were defeated, and both returned to live out their lives in Europe.

77. Mary of Modena, James's second wife, by Willem Wissing, c. 1685.

52

WILLIAM III

Born:	4 November 1650
Died:	8 March 1702
Reigned:	1689–1702
Parents:	William II of Nassau, Prince of Orange and Stadtholder of the United Provinces of the Netherlands, and Mary Stuart (daughter of King Charles I)
Married:	Mary Stuart, daughter of King James II (James Stuart, Duke of York)
Children:	None who survived
House:	Stuart/Orange
Illustration:	78. William III as a child

The significance of both the necessity and the outcome of the reign of William and Mary cannot be overstated. In terms of two prominent considerations – religion and political power – the acceptance of the dual monarchs from Holland to replace the rejected James II pointed the way to a future that allowed and encouraged the continued growth and evolution of England's constitutional monarchy. Parliament's vision of a Parliament-controlled monarch within a defined religious compatibility, coupled with the restrained yet effective administration of William and Mary, allowed England to prosper, while avoiding the more extreme religious and political upheavals that would plague France, Russia, and much of the rest of the European continent.

William reigned as a co-monarch with his wife Mary II (daughter of James II) from 1689 to 1694, and on his own until 1702. He had been born and raised in Holland, educated at Leiden University, and succeeded his father as Prince of Orange and Stadtholder (chief executive) of the Netherlands. He was a devout Protestant, experienced military commander, and shrewd manager of Dutch affairs. His overriding aim was to prevent a Catholic–French conquest of the Netherlands. To this end he married his first cousin, Mary Stuart, more than eleven years his junior and daughter of the Duke of York (the future King James II). This union created the hoped-for alliance of the Netherlands with England against the powerful French.

When James Stuart, the Duke of York, succeeded his brother Charles II as King of England in 1685, England was plunged into a religious and political dilemma that soon evolved into a crisis. Though a proven military commander and efficient administrator, James was also a strident Catholic, and like his father, Charles I, before him, he was a firm believer in the absolute power of monarchy. Parliament and its rules and requirements were to be abandoned or ignored, and though James's desire for religious equality rings well in our modern ear, it was a dangerous imposition at this point in time, resurrecting memories of violence from past religious wars and persecutions, and threatening similar horrors in the future. Since James's two daughters, and heirs to the throne, were both Protestants, it was hoped that time would remedy this situation. But when James's new wife, Mary of Modena, gave birth to a Catholic male heir, the situation became untenable.

Parliament responded with an invitation to William and Mary to enter England and claim the throne. This 'invited' army of invasion, personally led by William, arrived in late 1688 and was soon reinforced by enthusiastic popular support. The discredited King James II was forced to flee to France and abandon the throne to William and Mary. James's policy of summarily dismissing and replacing numerous civilian and military administrators on grounds of religious affiliation did much to encourage the withdrawal of support for his divisive cause.

In a near comedy of errors, James's departure was not only allowed, but peaceably encouraged and arranged by his would-be opponents. The peaceful nature of the bloodless coup, which would be named the Glorious Revolution, and the lack of reprisals on the part of William and Mary did much to temper the response and ease the acceptance for the removal of one king and installation of another. Along with James's removal came the new monarch's acceptance of several parliamentary stipulations that all future monarchs would be required to adhere to. These included the requirement for mandatory and frequent sessions of Parliament, and a specific listing of individual rights and royal limitations – the Bill of Rights of 1689, followed by the requirement for the sovereign to be a Protestant – putting an end to the threat of one 'national' religion replacing another due to a monarch's choice of faith.

As joint monarchs, William was to play the dominant role as policy maker in matters both foreign and domestic. Mary, though participating little in terms of governing or policy, was well-liked by the populace and contributed a lighter and more congenial personality to the dual monarchs' identity. Publicly, William was decidedly stiffer, more aloof, and lacking in charm. His foreign policy revolved around the maintenance of coalitions to provide protection for his native Holland, always under the threat from King Louis XIV's France. William's support of Protestant causes in Ireland and Scotland contributed to his becoming a hero to some and a tyrant to others. His initial triumph in Ireland at the Battle of the Boyne (1690), halted James II's attempt to re-enter Britain and regain his throne with the support of Catholic France, and firmly established (leading to endless future conflict) the position of Irish Protestants. James II also possessed support in Scotland from the Jacobites, and again this was backed with French aid, but this was eliminated by William's offering of a pardon to the Scottish clans. This approach proved effective, in spite of the massacre of numerous members of the MacDonald clan, of which William himself ordered an investigation.

William's Dutch wars resulted in considerable debt and debate, but as Parliament was now more and more the responsible author of these actions, it proved less controversial for William than it might otherwise have been. To meet the need of funding for these actions, the Bank of England was established in 1694, followed by the Bank of Scotland in 1695. 1694 was also the year of Mary's death due to smallpox, an event that William took very hard. He met his own death at age fifty-two in 1702 when his horse tripped on a mole hill, throwing William and breaking his collarbone. He died several days later from infection and was buried in Westminster Abbey. To his numerous opponents of Jacobite and Catholic persuasions, William's death was welcomed. To them, the little furry mole would always hold a place of honour as 'the little gentleman in black velvet'.

Certainly, the reasons behind and the consequences wrought by the arrival of William and Mary would have indelible ramifications on the future political and religious destiny of Great Britain. Their acceptance of a reduced authority, their restraint in the use of power, and the continued evolution of a constitutional monarchy would go far to providing England with a more stable platform to develop and prosper politically, financially, and globally in the coming centuries.

53

MARY II

Born:	30 April 1662
Died:	28 December 1694
Reigned:	1689–1694
Parents:	King James II (Stuart) and Anne Hyde
Married:	William III of Orange
Children:	Three or four, all stillborn
House:	Stuart
Illustration:	79. Mary II

Mary Stuart was the eldest daughter of James Stuart, Duke of York. Upon the death of James's brother, King Charles II, who had failed to produce a legitimate heir, James became king and Mary became the next in line to the throne. As king, James's open and strident imposition of his Catholic faith, both socially and politically, set in motion the sequence of events that rapidly escalated into his removal. As devout Protestants, Mary Stuart and her Dutch husband, William of Orange, were invited into England with the expressed intent of restoring a Protestant to the throne. Mary and William successfully filled this requirement and proceeded to reign jointly over England as co-monarchs.

Mary had been brought up as a Protestant at the insistence of her uncle, King Charles II. This was in keeping with Charles's desire to distance himself from any political or religious controversy, such as that which led to the trial and execution of his father, King Charles I. He kept his own religious inclination, Catholicism, in the background until his deathbed conversion – thereby preventing any political controversy such as that which would undo his openly proclaimed Catholic brother James.

When Mary was only fifteen she was married off to the Dutch Prince of Orange, William III, reportedly crying her eyes out at both the prospect of marrying the twelve-years-older and four-inches-shorter Dutchman, and of being required to move to the Netherlands. As it turned out, she enjoyed Holland, became quite popular with the people, and developed a deeply affectionate relationship with the prince. They produced at least two, and possibly three to four pregnancies, but all proved to be stillborn. The lack of an heir would deliver the crown to Mary's sister Anne, who also failed to produce a child that would live to adulthood – thus ending the Stuart dynasty.

Mary left most domestic and foreign policy to her husband William, although she did dutifully fulfil royal responsibilities during William's frequent absences while on military campaigns. She actively engaged architect Sir Christopher Wren in his splendid remodelling of Hampton Court Palace and is generally credited with the addition of the Serpentine Lake to the western end of Hyde Park. We also owe to her the creation of William and Mary College near Williamsburg, Virginia – the second-oldest college in the United States.

Mary was somewhat troubled by the removal of her father as King of England, but probably not to the extent as was her sister Anne. Mary was often out of sorts with her sister, particularly with regards to the subject of Anne's dedication to Sarah Churchill, wife of the distinguished General John Churchill, the future Duke of Marlborough. Churchill's defection from James II upon the arrival of the Prince of Orange was instrumental in the peaceful and rapid removal of James and subsequent replacement by William and Mary as co-monarchs. Churchill was later accused and imprisoned for *possibly* supporting a coup against William in order to place James II's son on the throne. Arousing this suspicion were the open opinions of Sarah and John Churchill, claiming that they had been denied adequate recognition and compensation for their support of William and Mary. This, however, became moot with the death of Mary in 1694 and William in 1702, allowing Anne as queen to exercise her complete confidence in Churchill, a faith well borne, as he proceeded to win numerous and incomparable victories on the Continent against Louis XIV's France.

Mary was only thirty-two years old when she died of smallpox in 1694. She was buried in Westminster Abbey. It was a loss most deeply felt by William. Mary's politically tranquil return to England and assumption of the throne, coupled with her and her husband's moderate and successful reign, allowed England to peaceably advance into a more Parliament-oriented monarchy. William and Mary's acceptance of the English Bill of Rights (1689) and the qualifications for royal succession continued England's peaceful transition to an ever-evolving and expanding constitutional monarchy. This form of government would lead England to a brilliant future of wealth and success. It was indeed a Glorious Revolution.

80. The coronation of William and Mary.
Opposite: 81. Mary II by Peter Lely.

54

ANNE

Born:	6 February 1665
Died:	1 August 1714
Reigned:	1702–1714
Parents:	King James II (Stuart) and Anne Hyde
Married:	Prince George of Denmark
Children:	At least seventeen pregnancies, of which five resulted in a live birth. Of these five, only two lived beyond a year: Mary (1685–1687) and William (1689–1700)
House:	Stuart
Illustration:	82. A statue of Anne outside St Paul's Cathedral

The reign of Queen Anne can be looked at from two perspectives: either she was wise enough to allow England's growing power and prosperity to bloom by staying out of the way, or, England was able to continue her growth in power because Anne recognised able leaders. Either way, although Anne personally lacked intellectual depth and ambition, her short twelve-year reign saw England win great victories on the battlefields of Europe and witnessed achievements in science, art and architecture. The country also continued evolving her domestic political system into a constitutional monarchy. And in 1707, under the Act of Union, England and Scotland officially became the United Kingdom.

Anne was the last English monarch from the House of Stuart. Like her sister Mary, she was the daughter of King James II, who had been removed from the throne in 1688 during the Glorious Revolution. She had also been raised a Protestant at the insistence of her uncle, King Charles II, in order to convince Parliament of his commitment to Protestantism after his restoration. Anne was devoted to the Church of England, but she did feel remorse at the removal of her divisively Catholic father from the throne and his lifelong banishment to France. This had caused a rift with her sister, as Anne felt Mary lacked sufficient sympathy for their father. Mary in turn disapproved of Anne's close relationship with Sarah Churchill, and the two sisters did not speak to each other for the last few years of Mary's reign.

Anne was never healthy and suffered from numerous illnesses, including severe gout, rheumatism and obesity. She endured at least seventeen pregnancies, only five of which produced a living child, and only two of those lived beyond one year. This was probably due to her overall poor health and her overindulgent eating and drinking habits. She was unable to walk up the aisle at her coronation and her mobility was frequently limited – she had to be carried in a wheelchair or sedan chair. Anne also drank to excess, in particular brandy, inspiring her nickname, 'Brandy Nan'. Supposedly, her coffin was in the shape of a cube.

Poorly educated and not interested in literature, the arts, or music, Anne preferred games, gambling, and hunting in the forest. Her husband, Prince George of Denmark, was equally modest in both intellectual background and pursuits, although he certainly played his part adequately when it came to the production of heirs – even if the children did not survive. But Anne was friendly, gentle, and well-intentioned; her down-to-earth style made her popular with the people. She displayed a strong sense of duty to her position, and had a warm-hearted personality that belied her pain from illness and lack of childbearing success. In 1700, the death of her one surviving child, the eleven-year-old William, brought grief to her and her husband. Prince George's death in 1708 was another great sadness, as they had been very close.

Anne took her royal role seriously. She attempted to attend cabinet meetings once or twice a week, as much as any monarch before or since, and although her actual contributions were limited, her attendance reflected her sense of duty. Anne was the last English monarch to attend a meeting of the Privy Council and the last to refuse a Bill passed by Parliament. Anne relied on the competent Sidney Godolphin to administer domestic policy and John Churchill to be her Captain-General in England's European wars with Louis XIV's formidable armies. Her choice of Churchill, the husband of her closest friend, Sarah Churchill, was to have a huge impact upon European history. Churchill had been one of James II's leading officers but had supported William and Mary against James during the Glorious Revolution. Churchill achieved brilliant success on the battlefields of Europe, winning great victories at Blenheim, Oudenarde, and Ramilles during the War of Spanish Succession (1702–1708).

Sarah (Jennings) Churchill had been Anne's friend since childhood, and Anne had come to rely upon her for everything from companionship to advice. Sarah had been involved with Anne's support of the invasion of William and Mary and the removal of her father, James II, from the throne. When Anne became queen, Sarah became Anne's Mistress of the Robes and Keeper of the Privy Purse, two powerful royal household positions, and John became her leading army commander. As Duke and Duchess of Marlborough they would build a spectacular mansion, Blenheim Palace, at Woodstock in Oxfordshire.

The relationship with the Churchills ended in 1710–1711, when Sarah and Anne's friendship broke down, followed by the dismissal of Sarah and John from their respective positions of rank. This coincided with the ongoing cost and unpopularity of the long-running War of Spanish Succession, and the gradual growth of the rival Whig and Tory political parties – the formation of which ran parallel to the rise in Parliament's policy-determining power. As the Churchills leant their support to the Whigs and continuation of the war, this inevitably collided with Anne's more Tory-leaning hopes of an end to the war and its expenses.

Sarah Churchill was replaced by her cousin, Lady Abigail Masham, who assumed the role of faithful companion through Anne's later years. Anne suffered increasingly through her declining final years, experiencing grief at the death of her husband in 1708, enduring further deteriorating health, and feeling anguish at her fruitless attempts to persuade her half-brother James ('The Old Pretender' to the throne and son of James II) to renounce his Catholic faith in order to be placed back into the line of succession.

Anne died in 1714, probably from a stroke, and was buried at Westminster Abbey. Anne's reign had seen the passage of the Act of Union (1707) that united England and Scotland into the United Kingdom, grand military victories under Marlborough, the capture of the strategic base of Gibraltar in 1704, and the rise of English trade throughout the world, with its accompanying wealth and possibilities for global economic and military dominance in the future. Anne knighted Isaac Newton in 1705, celebrated the architectural splendours of the completed remodelling of Hampton Court Palace and the completion of St Paul's Cathedral in London by Christopher Wren, promoted the benefaction for the extravagantly baroque exuberance of Blenheim Palace, and comfortably adjusted to the role of queen that was being shaped to a constitutional monarchy. Easy to ridicule and ignore, Anne displayed a lack of pretension, coupled with an unashamed acceptance and a grasp of the ordinary, which helped provide England with a secure political base to engage, accept, and promote her unlimited potential for the future.

55

GEORGE I

Born:	28 May 1660
Died:	11 June 1727
Reigned:	1714–1727
Parents:	Ernest Augustus, Elector of Hanover, and Sophia, daughter of Elizabeth of Bohemia (daughter of King James I)
Married:	Sophia Dorothea of Celle
Children:	One son, George I and one daughter. Three illegitimate children
House:	Hanover
Illustration:	83. George I

George I became the first monarch from the House of Hanover. He assumed the throne in 1714 on the death of Queen Anne. There were perhaps fifty Roman Catholic relatives more closely related to Anne than George, but the Act of Settlement in 1701 strictly required the throne to be passed on to the nearest Protestant relation. George's grandmother, Elizabeth of Bohemia, had been the daughter of James I, King of England. George's mother, Sophia, the heir to the throne, had died just months before. It was this line of Protestants dating back to the era of Queen Elizabeth I that placed George of Hanover in line for the throne. George had previously visited England, but spoke little or no English, and clearly retained his distinctive German habits, culture and political outlook. Even after inheriting the throne of England, he never ceased to return regularly to Hanover, finally dying and being buried in his native Hanover in 1727.

As a youth, George received military training and gained experience in the Dutch and Turkish wars. He had visited England as early as 1680 to meet and perhaps marry Anne, but nothing came of the meeting. George later married Sophia Dorothea of Celle and had two children, but that marriage dissolved when both acquired lovers. George took his mistress to England when he became king and ennobled her as the Duchess of Kendal. He wasn't so kind with his wife. Her lover was found strangled and George was rumoured to be behind the murder. His wife was held in captivity for the rest of her life at Ahlden Castle in Lower Saxony Germany, unbelievably for the next thirty years!

When he arrived in England in 1714 to assume the throne, George spoke French in order to communicate. His coronation at Westminster Abbey was conducted in Latin so that he could understand the proceedings. The language and cultural barrier between George and his parliamentary government meant that a single chief administrator conducted most of the king's business in terms of finance and policy. This man appeared in the person of Robert Walpole, who, as the king's main or 'prime' minister, became the conduit between George and Parliament, which Walpole more or less controlled. By 1721, as head of Parliament's dominant Whig party as well as Chancellor of the

Exchequer, Walpole held a commanding position in government and was setting a precedent for the future administration of government in England. The king would no longer personally debate with Parliament, but would rely more and more on his chief or 'prime' minister to obtain money to fight wars, build a palace, or maintain his court. Walpole held this post until 1742, through the reign of George I and into that of George II, establishing the office that would gradually grow into England's version of a chief executive.

In 1715–1716, early in his reign, George was able to subdue a Scottish rebellion that attempted to put James II's Catholic son on the throne. It was quickly crushed and James, 'The Old Pretender', returned to France.

George was already fifty-four years old when crowned, and was never fully embraced by the populace. He was wise enough to keep a low profile in terms of not interfering in English politics and culture. His love for Hanover never left him, and he travelled back to Hanover as frequently as possible; he was openly at his happiest while visiting his native land. He quarrelled bitterly with his son, the future George II, and the two maintained virtual parallel courts in London.

George took the throne at a delicate moment, the time of the transition between the Stuart and Hanover dynasties, which was encompassed by the ever thorny question of the religion of the monarch. To England's governing credit it was resolved peacefully. George handled his duties with sensible restraint and left a firm and stable situation for the future Hanovers to reign over, along with the continued rise of Parliament actually to govern. It was while visiting Hanover in 1727 that George fell ill, suffered a stroke, and died. He was buried in Hanover at Leineschlosskirche. His body was later reinterred at Herrenhausen, Hanover in 1957.

56

GEORGE II

Born:	30 October 1683
Died:	25 October 1760
Reigned:	1727–1760
Parents:	George I and Sophia Dorothea of Celle
Married:	Caroline of Ansbach
Children:	Two sons: Frederick, Prince of Wales, and William, Duke of Cumberland. Five daughters: Anne, Amelia, Caroline, Mary, and Louisa
House:	Hanover
Illustration:	84. George II

Probably better known for his faults than his strengths, George II is perhaps one of the most underrated of all the British monarchs. George II presided over the creation of a global British empire that was to dominate the world economically, geographically and militarily for nearly the next two centuries. While not necessarily playing an active role in creating this environment, George II was wise and astute enough largely to avoid meddling and let those in charge carry on with their schemes and dreams. Though not without behavioural failings, George II largely avoided embarrassing himself socially or politically on the scale of George IV or Charles I. Indeed, militarily he showed great bravery and was recognised for his battlefield leadership, and there are greater weaknesses than being boring or pedestrian in one's pursuits.

George I had reigned as the first British king from the House of Hanover. George II was his only son and, like his father, was born and raised in the German state of Hanover. The future George II began practising English when his father ascended the throne in 1714, and the two Georges moved to England. By this time, the younger George was married (in 1705), had fathered several children, and had actively participated in the War of Spanish Succession, where he was lauded by the British commander, the Duke of Marlborough, for his valour at the Battle of Oudenarde (1708). After 1714 George II lived mainly in England, though he often returned to Hanover. He became king in 1727, reigning until his death in 1760. He is the last British monarch to be buried at Westminster Abbey.

George II endured a turbulent relationship with his father. In 1694, when George II was only ten years old, his father, George I, imprisoned his own wife, Sophia, for alleged infidelity, forbidding her the right to see her son. George I also generally rejected any potential talents his son showed, and withheld from him appointments of any significant responsibility. However, during the first two years of George I's reign, the younger George successfully served as an interpreter during meetings of the Cabinet and Privy Council. He also served as Regent during George I's frequent returns to Hanover, of which he remained Elector General. This working relationship came to an end in 1717 when father and son had a significant falling out. Ironically, these disagreements encouraged George II to become more deeply involved in English society. Nevertheless, George II, like his father before him, always relished his visits to Hanover, where he too later assumed the post of Elector General.

George II was short and fierce, and according to his Vice-Chamberlain, Lord Hervey, 'grudged the English their riches as well as their liberties, and thought them overpaid'. He cared little for reading and research, which frequently put him at a political disadvantage in his relations with his strong-willed ministers such as Robert Walpole, William Pitt, and the Pelhams, Henry and Thomas (Duke of Newcastle). He enjoyed music and was a strong supporter and patron of composer Fredrick Handel. The tradition of standing for the 'Hallelujah Chorus' during Handel's *Messiah* has traditionally been attributed to George II rising during its rousing, show-stopping performance, but this has never been substantially documented.

George II generally refrained from domestic politics, allowing his 'prime' minister to handle these affairs. He showed an awareness of European matters, especially when it came to supporting England's participation in European wars that protected or benefited the state of Hanover. In 1742, during the War of Austrian Succession, he led the British Army against the French at the victorious Battle of Dettingen – the last time an English monarch would personally command an army on the field of battle.

George II's marriage to Caroline of Ansbach was successful on both a personal and social level. Caroline was known for her wit and political acumen. Early in George I's reign, Caroline acted effectively in lieu of George I's imprisoned wife. Later, following the father-and-son rupture, Caroline and the future George II conducted a parallel competing royal court at the Prince of Wales's London residence, Leicester House. This had far-reaching repercussions. Given George I's inability to communicate in English, he relied even more upon his leading minister, Robert Walpole. This in turn encouraged and allowed Walpole wider latitude to determine domestic and foreign policy. Walpole's twenty-one-year service as lead (or 'prime') minister established the power and position of the post that we today refer to as the Prime Minister. So essential and pervasive was Walpole's position that, upon assuming the throne, George II retained him as his chief minister for the next fifteen years.

George II, though he actively enjoyed numerous mistresses, was otherwise devoted to his wife and insisted on their tombs being adjoined in Westminster Abbey. They had two noteworthy sons among their eight children: Frederick, Prince of Wales (1707–1751), and William, Duke of Cumberland (1721–1765). Both George II and Caroline detested the Prince of Wales, and Frederick obliged the situation by following in his father's footsteps and maintaining an alternative royal court, again at Leicester House! Frederick's court commanded London's social scene as it completely outshone the king's in glamour and prestige. The prince, who died before his father, also produced nine children, including the future King George III. But William was clearly the king's favourite, and led the military rout of 'Bonny' Prince Charles Stuart's Jacobite Rebellion of 1745. Cumberland (nicknamed 'Butcher Cumberland') led the British Army in their annihilation of the Scots at the Battle of Culloden (1746) – the last major battle fought on British soil. The elimination and execution of the Jacobites and their failed attempt to restore the Catholic Stuarts to power marked the end of any hope that the Stuart line would ever regain the throne of England.

In sum, George II saw England gain India under Robert Clive, defeat the French in Canada at Quebec, and dominate the high seas, while George himself maintained a firm Protestant grip on the British throne with the complete eviction of the Jacobite threat. George would quarrel with Walpole, Pitt, and the Pelhams, but in the end would rely upon them to run government. He presided over England acquiring an undreamed-of empire of immense size, scope and wealth, while unwittingly establishing the tradition of a parliamentary chief executive that would evolve into the position of Prime Minister. His common sense allowed these developments to grow and to flourish, setting the stage for Great Britain to emerge as an imperial world power for virtually the next two centuries.

57

GEORGE III

Born:	4 June 1738
Died:	29 January 1820
Reigned:	1760–1820
Parents:	Frederick Louis, Prince of Wales, and Princess Augusta of Saxe-Coburg-Gotha
Married:	Charlotte Sophia of Mecklenburg-Strelitz
Children:	Fifteen. Nine sons: notably George IV and William IV, plus Frederick, Edward, Ernest, Augustus, Octavius, Alfred, and Adolphus. Six daughters: Charlotte, Augusta, Elizabeth, Mary, Amelia, and Sophia
House:	Hanover
Illustration:	85. George III

The first British-born king since James II, George III reigned for fifty-nine years, although his later years were marred by bouts of ill health and mental illness. In his final tragic decade, due to his incapacity to function coherently, he was replaced by his eldest son George, who served as Prince Regent.

George III was the first of the Hanoverian monarchs to speak English as a native, a fact of which he was quite proud. He was fond of simple pleasures and pastimes, and enjoyed his nickname of 'farmer George', due to his happiness in farming. Stubborn and not bursting with great intellect, he was, however, hard-working, diligent in his duties and morally virtuous – he displayed none of the extravagant financial excesses or marital infidelities with which many of his Hanoverian relations seemed infected.

George succeeded his grandfather, George II, in 1760, his father, Frederick, Prince of Wales, having died in 1751. George III's first order of business was to end the costly Seven Years' War (the French and Indian War in North America), by replacing the former administration of George II. The former king and his war-minded ministers had pursued the war to England's great imperial advantage, although at great financial expense. George was keen to appoint his own government, end the war, and pay down the national debt. This was to have dramatic consequences.

George III was the last of the English monarchs to have a real say in the selection and dismissal of his government. He chose to rid himself of the empire-building coalition surrounding William Pitt (the Elder) and his Whig associates, and replaced them with his own favourites such as John Stuart, Earl of Bute, and later Frederick, Lord North. In these ministerial manipulations George succeeded, but in practical terms of policy he failed. Bute was despised by Parliament, and North, though loyal and dedicated, was inadequate. Bute ended the Seven Years' War, but resigned under pressure, giving way to George Grenville, whose prudently efficient policy of placing taxes on England's North American colonies drastically backfired into a rebellion and war that led to the thirteen colonies declaring independence. The more pragmatic Pitt faction desired to retain the thirteen rebellious colonies at all costs, but George stubbornly insisted on enforcing his will upon the colonies, thereby ensuring their resistance, and in the end, their independence. George cannot necessarily be blamed for losing the colonies, but he certainly was responsible for the intransigence that prevented an earlier reconciliation, which might have avoided war.

George also stubbornly clung to his intolerant Irish policy in reaction to Prime Minister William Pitt (the Younger)'s proposals to grant emancipation to Catholics, be more inclusive with the Catholic Irish in government, and be less repressive in their treatment. Unfortunately, George was adamant in his rejection of these suggestions and Pitt resigned over the issue.

Pitt the Younger served two terms as George III's Prime Minister, 1783–1801 and 1804–1806, and remained his loyal supporter. Both Pitt and George feared the crisis of the French Revolution in 1789 and the ensuing war that engulfed Europe for nearly three decades. Pitt, and England, became the dogged opponent of Napoleon Bonaparte, defiantly refusing to concede defeat in the face of repeated setbacks. Pitt tragically died an early death in 1806, before being able to savour victory in 1815 with the Duke of Wellington's decisive victory over Napoleon at the Battle of Waterloo.

Nor was George III in a position to enjoy the victory; having recovered from earlier bouts of mental illness, by 1810 his condition had deteriorated into hopeless dementia. Nearly blind, deaf, and out of touch with reality, George was confined to his rooms at Windsor Castle and taken care of by his wife, Charlotte. His son George was declared Prince Regent in 1811, and became king at George III's death in 1820. Medical experts today believe that George III's condition was due to an inherited disease known as porphyria, a disease of the nervous system, inducing fits, psychosis and other mental symptoms as exhibited by George.

George's marriage to Charlotte of Mecklenburg-Strelitz was stable and enduring, producing fifteen children, including two future kings. Charlotte died in 1818. They were married for fifty-seven years and are buried together in St George's Chapel at Windsor Castle.

86. Queen Charlotte.

58

GEORGE IV

Born:	12 August 1762
Died:	26 June 1830
Reigned:	1820–1830
Parents:	George III and Charlotte Sophia
Married:	(1.) Maria (Smythe) Fitzherbert, secretly married and later annulled, and (2.) Caroline of Brunswick
Children:	(2.) One daughter, Charlotte. And at least two illegitimate children
House:	Hanover
Illustration:	87. George IV

An eclectic mix of extravagance, foolishness, charm, flamboyance, and an overindulgence in all things self-destructive; these features, along with more, mostly negative, traits, contribute to establishing George IV as a classic study in irresponsibility. As king, he was anything but a leader. He had no vision as a monarch, nor any interest in government whatsoever, other than for it to pay his bills and support his hedonistic lifestyle. George squandered a fortune in his compulsively conspicuous pursuit of the fashionable during the period known as the Regency. His trendy allegiance to fashion and his addiction to pouring enormous sums of money – the money from his nation's treasury – into such fantastic flights of fancy as the Royal Pavilion at Brighton, only further underscore his reckless and selfish abuse of his exalted position. He relied on everyone else to pay for his profligate spending, and contributed little or nothing to his nation, family and friends, or in the end, to himself. He died grossly obese, virtually friendless, and without a legitimate heir.

George IV was the eldest son of George III. As the Prince of Wales he was bright, witty, and vain, setting trends for elegant fashion, fine dining, and frivolous behaviour. He had a multitude of mistresses, but eventually settled on the twice-widowed Maria Fitzherbert, whom he secretly – and illegally, due to royal and legal obligations – married in 1785. In order to satisfy his enormous debts, George cut a deal with Parliament and agreed to *officially* marry Caroline of Brunswick in 1795. They had one daughter, Charlotte, in 1796. Unfortunately, George despised everything about Caroline and wanted nothing to do with her. Caroline's returning presence at his coronation would later further plague and embarrass him.

George enjoyed spending time with his daughter Charlotte, who became quite popular as an heiress. Charlotte later married, bore a stillborn child, and died immediately following the childbirth in 1817. George was devastated by her death. This left George, now fifty-four years old, without an heir.

The period 1793–1815 saw England heavily and expensively embroiled in war with France. George III had grown increasingly unstable mentally, and in 1811, his son George, Prince of Wales, was declared Prince Regent to act in place of his incapacitated father. The Napoleonic Wars with France placed a great strain on England both financially and militarily, but through persistence and determination, Britain and her allies emerged victorious. The Prince Regent's contribution was his continued dedication to the highly celebrated achievements of architecture, fashion, furniture and art that lends its name to the Regency period. Numerous examples of this period's achievements remain today. The remodelling of Buckingham Palace and Windsor Castle, the Royal Pavilion at Brighton, the terraces around Regent's Park, and Regent's Street itself, along with the striking paintings at Windsor Castle commemorating the leading figures of the Napoleonic Wars – all speak to the splendid artistic creativity of the period. We can attribute much of this to George's exuberant and expensive desire for artistic achievement.

Upon George III's death in 1820, the Prince Regent succeeded to the throne, his coronation providing an opportunity to further indulge his lavish commitment to pomp and splendour. It was a spectacular ceremony that degenerated into royal farce. The rejected queen consort, Caroline, appeared uninvited at Westminster Abbey, completely infuriating the new king. George not only rejected her participation in the ceremony, but repeatedly insisted that the pathetic Caroline be barred from even entering the building. Already in an unhealthy state, the humiliated fifty-three-year-old uncrowned queen died a few months later in 1821 and was buried in her native Brunswick, Germany; a tragic end to an embarrassing story of royal misbehaviour.

George IV temporarily won back some royal respect with his colourful visits to Ireland and Scotland, as the first Hanoverian monarch to do this. His ability to pose and posture in the trappings of grand settings and ostentatious ceremonies was something at which George could excel. Unfortunately, as the 1820s progressed, his continuously selfish and dissolute lifestyle only further impugned his reputation. Increasingly obese, George's health deteriorated and he descended into a state of broken spirits and illness, dividing his time between Windsor Castle and his magnificent retreat at Brighton, while living with his final mistress, Lady Elizabeth Conyngham.

The formerly supremely elegant gentleman of the Regency was now hopelessly dissipated and corpulent. George died in 1830 at age sixty-seven. He was buried at St George's Chapel, Windsor Castle.

88. A cartoon by Robert Cruikshank. George IV in a rage against his family members.

WILLIAM IV

Born:	21 August 1765
Died:	20 June 1837
Reigned:	1830–1837
Parents:	George III and Charlotte Sophia
Married:	Princess Adelaide of Saxe-Meinigen
Children:	None who survived infancy. Ten illegitimate children by Dorothea (Bland) Jordan
House:	Hanover
Illustration:	89. William IV

William, Duke of Clarence, was the third son of King George III and went into the Royal Navy. It was never suspected that he would succeed as king, and he was known as the 'Sailor King'. He was a friend of Horatio Nelson, and gave the bride away at Nelson's wedding. In 1811 he was made honorary Admiral of the Fleet.

After leaving the Navy, William began a twenty-one-year affair with actress Dorothea (Bland) Jordan that produced ten children, all of whom were later ennobled upon William's succession to the throne. This arrangement ended abruptly in 1811 and Dorothea returned to the stage. With a lack of potential legitimate heirs in the Hanover stable, William married a German princess, Adelaide of Saxe-Meinigen. Although a happy relationship, it did not create any children that survived to adulthood.

Later, William abolished the use of the cat-o-nine tails, except for in cases of mutiny, and commissioned England's first steam warship. In 1828 William resigned his position in the Royal Navy, as it became clear that he would probably inherit the throne. William's older brother Frederick, Duke of York, had died in 1827, placing William next in line, and in 1830 upon the death of King George IV, William became king.

During William's tenure as king, Parliament passed Prime Minister Charles Grey's Great Reform Bill of 1832; this landmark legislation eliminated rotten boroughs and expanded the right of vote to more citizens. Though at first adamantly opposing the legislation, William eventually gave in and grudgingly accepted the more inclusive notion of suffrage. The abolition of slavery in the British Empire followed in 1834. Though William was hardly spearheading these movements of liberalisation, it did indicate that he and the monarchy were coming to grips, even if reluctantly, with the pressures and terms of a more enlightened modern age.

This budding new age can be summed up in the words of William IV. He remarked, 'I have my view of things, and I tell them to my ministers. If they do not adopt them, I cannot help it. I have done my duty.'

William was fond of his niece and heir to the throne, Victoria, daughter of William's deceased younger brother Edward, Duke of Kent. William lived long enough to ensure that Victoria assumed the throne without a regent. He died at Windsor Castle in 1837, and was buried at St George's Chapel, Windsor Castle. His wife Adelaide, whom Adelaide, Australia, is named after, is buried with him.

VICTORIA

Born:	24 May 1819
Died:	22 January 1901
Reigned:	1837–1901
Parents:	Edward, 1st Duke of Kent (George III's fourth son), and Victoria of Saxe-Coburg
Married:	Prince Albert of Saxe-Coburg-Gotha
Children:	Four sons: Albert (Edward VII), Alfred, Arthur and Leopold. Five daughters: Victoria, Louise, Beatrice, and Helena
House:	Hanover
Illustration:	90. Victoria

Queen Victoria was on the throne for nearly sixty-four years. Her reign rejuvenated the monarchy, which had suffered a serious decline in reputation over the previous fifty years of Hanover rule. Preceding Victoria had been George III, who had drifted in and out of mental illness for the last two decades of his reign before completely succumbing to it; his son George IV, who hopelessly tarnished not only his own name but also the monarchy's with his scandalous behaviour and profligate spending; and Victoria's immediate predecessor, the amiable and pedestrian William IV, who at least had the good sense to keep out of the way until Victoria assumed the throne in 1837. Victoria's long reign then saw the transition of Great Britain into the most powerful empire on earth; her vast economic and colonial empire came to stretch around the planet. Born into a 'horse and buggy era', she lived and reigned to see the rise of railroads, transoceanic steamships, telegraph and telephone communication, the birth of photography and radio, and the onset of the automobile. It was a breathtaking advance in science and industry.

Parallel to the restoration of the monarchy's reputation and the spectacular growth of the British Empire was the acceptance of the monarch's lack of influence in political decisions. Following George III's illness, George IV's incompetence and William IV's irrelevance, the reign of Victoria clearly demonstrated that the role of the constitutional British monarch was ceremonial at best and perhaps due for extinction at worst. British monarchs now reigned – they no longer ruled. Within that context, however, there was still much that a clever, enthusiastic and dynamic monarch could do to justify his or her position and benefit the nation.

Victoria, the daughter of Edward, Duke of Kent, succeeded to the throne in 1837, due to the lack of surviving legitimate heirs from the children of George III. Victoria had been raised in a sheltered environment and assumed the throne at the age of eighteen. Her early instruction into foreign and domestic politics came from Prime Minister William Lamb, Lord Melbourne. Melbourne made it his personal mission to spend hours patiently chatting with and instructing the young queen in the ways of politics and the world. In 1840, Victoria married Prince Albert of the German state of Saxe-Coburg-Gotha, and they enjoyed a vigorous production of nine children within the next seventeen years. Besides having a generous talent for procreation, Albert was also a prominent figure when it came to many of the couple's genuinely outstanding and long-lasting contributions to the nation.

Albert was an intelligent, well-educated and hard-working young man who, besides providing moral rectitude for the monarchy, was energetic and open-minded to innovation and progress. He spearheaded the 1851 Great Exhibition in London's Hyde Park, a world's fair of invention and modern industry that was wildly popular and financially successful. The main exhibition hall was the glass-and-steel Crystal Palace, a modern wonder of structural engineering. The profits from this enterprise were ploughed back into the purchase of property and the establishment of the museum campus in South Kensington that features the Victoria and Albert Museum, the Science Museum, and Royal Albert Hall, among other noteworthy institutions of science and learning. Albert also introduced the Yuletide tradition of the Christmas tree from his native Germany. It was Albert's early death from typhoid fever in 1861, at only forty-two, that so devastated Victoria and plunged her into a life-long period of mourning.

Victoria's reign encompassed ten prime ministers. She enjoyed a father–daughter-like relationship with Lord Melbourne, learned to get along with and respect Robert Peel, but abhorred Lord (John) Russell and Lord Palmerston (Henry Temple), referring to them as 'those two dreadful old men'. Benjamin Disraeli charmed her completely and made her Empress of India, while his erstwhile opponent William Gladstone incurred her agitation and irritation. It was Gladstone who attempted to scold her into again making more public appearances in order to reconnect with her subjects; after all, she was the queen. But Victoria resented Gladstone's manner, both personally and politically.

During the deepest period of Victoria's mourning she seemed to have forfeited some favour with the populace, but the celebration of her Golden and Diamond Jubilees regained much of her lost popularity, as Victoria and her 'era' became identified as the symbol of Great Britain's imperial success. She did not prefer Buckingham Palace, but chose Windsor Castle, Osborne House on the Isle of Wight, and Balmoral Castle in Scotland as her principal residences. It was at Osborne House, in 1901, that Victoria died. She had become the 'Grandmother of Europe'; she was directly or through marriage related to the royal houses of Germany, Russia, Norway, Greece, Denmark, Sweden, Romania, and Belgium.

Victoria was buried beside her beloved Albert at the Royal Mausoleum at Frogmore, in Great Windsor Park.

91. An older Queen Victoria.

61

EDWARD VII

Born:	9 November 1841
Died:	6 May 1910
Reigned:	1901–1910
Parents:	Prince Albert of Saxe-Coburg-Gotha and Queen Victoria
Married:	Alexandria of Denmark
Children:	Three sons: Albert, Prince of Wales, George, Duke of York (King George V) and Alexander. Three daughters: Louise, Victoria, and Maud
House:	Saxe-Coburg-Gotha
Illustration:	92. Edward VII

A king who has an age named after him, Edward VII was a monarch with a large appetite for food, wine, women, travel, gambling, racing horses, and fashionable living. Created Prince of Wales in 1841, he then waited sixty years to attain the throne. By the time he became king he had spent his youth and adult life in endless pursuit of pleasure and passion. Denied by his mother, Queen Victoria, the opportunity to participate in any meaningful role of government, Edward resorted to a career of epicurean joy, beautiful mistresses, and endless travel to European resorts and faraway locales. His fashion, lifestyle, and scandals became the subject of constant gossip, criticism, embarrassment, and – let's be honest – envy!

Looking back from the present it all seems rather natural – a vigorous youth of reckless and excited libido, generous wealth and privilege, combined with rank, position, and boundless opportunity, and virtually nothing to do except follow the allure of recreational desires. This was in particularly stark contrast to the sombre and dull routine of Queen Victoria's dreary decades of mourning that persisted through the second half of the nineteenth century. But unlike other hedonist monarchs, Edward was supremely visible, charming, affable, fun-loving, and mindful of his duties. When presented with responsibilities, and finally able to assume them, he acquitted himself admirably.

Edward was born in Buckingham Palace, the eldest son of Queen Victoria and her consort Prince Albert of Saxe-Coburg-Gotha. He attended both Oxford and Cambridge, but, although bright, was an indifferent student at best. Early on, Edward's interests were inclined to carousing, drinking, and womanising. It was in this regard that Edward's father, Prince Albert, visited him at Cambridge concerning his recent peccadilloes, and fell ill. Albert died shortly thereafter from typhoid fever, and it was this unexpectedly early death at age forty-two that Victoria unreasonably not only blamed Edward for, but for which she also never forgave him.

Certainly, Edward's lifestyle was legendary. It featured dozens of mistresses and countless other incidental liaisons. His well-known mistresses included actress Lillie Langtry, Countess of Warwick

Daisy Greville, and Mrs George Keppel (Alice Edmonstone), who was brought to Edward's deathbed to be beside him as he died in 1910 and who is the great-grandmother of Camilla Parker Bowles, the current wife of Charles, Prince of Wales. Edward had married Princess Alexandra, daughter of King Christian IX of Denmark, in 1863. The union produced six children, including the future King George V, and the couple enjoyed a stable and mutually agreeable marriage in spite of Edward's numerous paramours. It was by Queen Alexandra's request that Mrs Keppel was summoned to Edward's bedside as he lay dying.

Edward loved travelling and delighted in visiting such far-flung locations as India, Canada, and the United States. He regularly made frequent trips to Europe, where he engaged his habitual preoccupation with fine food, gambling, and hunting. He is often credited with making Monte Carlo the 'in' place to be, and to be seen. From fine cigars, usually a dozen a day, to elegant fashion, Edward sought the best and set trends. His racehorses won numerous races and events including the Derby, and his support of the arts and sciences included the founding of the Royal College of Music in 1883. Edward was keen to cut ribbons and inaugurate grand openings of such new projects as Tower Bridge and the Thames Embankment – he relished the spotlight, looked the part, and basked in the attention. It was positive publicity to a public that had endured four decades of Queen Victoria's withdrawal and austere behaviour when in private mourning. The hearty English Sunday dinner tradition of roast beef with horseradish sauce and roast potatoes, topped off with Yorkshire pudding, is said to have been inspired by Edward's fondness for the meal. Of course, indulging his appetite led to his wide girth, which required the lower button of his waistcoat (vest) to be left unbuttoned – a fashion that was copied and continues to this day.

In his short, ten-year reign as king, Edward was finally able to contribute on a broader scale. He resumed the practice of personally opening Parliament, a tradition that the reclusive Victoria had declined. He was a strong advocate of maintaining a superior modern naval force, improving the Army medical service branch, and reforming the operation and preparation of the Army in general – all factors that would bear fruit in the coming First World War. He is often given credit for having an influential role in European foreign affairs and for the strengthening of ties with France in opposition to the rising threat of the German Empire, but most sources attest to only a superficial participation – detail and in-depth research were never Edward's strong points.

His overriding success and contribution to the nation was the restoration of the popularity of the monarchy following the long and melancholy reign of his mother. Edward's charismatic personality, and willingness to enthusiastically project this personality onto the public stage as a larger-than-life figure, was a refreshing contrast to the continual funereal gloom of his predecessor. The consequence was the evolution and survival of the British monarchy during the calamitous next decade of world history – a decade that witnessed the downfall, or violent death, of nearly every European imperial throne. The Edwardian Age was truly a time of aristocratic elegance and extravagance, personified by its namesake, Edward VII. It was an age about to end forever.

62

GEORGE V

Born:	3 June 1865
Died:	20 January 1936
Reigned:	1910–1936
Parents:	Prince Albert Edward (later Edward VII) and Princess Alexandra of Denmark
Married:	Mary of Teck
Children:	Five sons: Edward VIII, George VI (Albert), Henry, Edward and John. One daughter: Mary
House:	Windsor
Illustration:	93. George V

Another younger son who ended up becoming king due to the death of his older brother, George V had enjoyed a career in the Royal Navy, similar to William IV. His steady personality, straightforward character, and devotion to duty endeared him to his nation and set a standard for the image of a constitutional monarch in the modern world. During George's reign many truly significant events transpired: the great liberal legislation under Herbert Asquith and David Lloyd George, the First World War and with it the death of the Russian, German, and Austrian empires along with the collapse of their monarchial governments, the maturing of the Labour Party, the Great Depression of the 1930s, and the rise of Adolf Hitler's Nazi Germany and the looming Second World War. It was a portentous era in world history, and George's dignified maturity provided an understated calm to the events that were engulfing the world.

George's background as an officer in the Royal Navy had taken him around the world and provided him with an opportunity for exposure to a wide range of worldly experiences. However, his personal compass remained fixed on England and the aristocratic country life that he enjoyed so well. His wife and family, hunting on his estate at Sandringham, and stamp collecting – these remained his passions for life.

George got along well with his father, King Edward VII, even though he never emulated Edward's lifestyle of fine wining and dining while romancing a stable of elegant ladies. Edward shared state papers with George and did his best to help prepare him for his future kingship. They remained forever close. George became heir in 1892 on the death of his older brother Albert, Duke of Clarence, and succeeded his father as king in 1910. He was married to his older brother's fiancée, Mary of Teck, in 1893, and they went on to have five sons and one daughter.

During the First World War, when all things German became suspect, George and other members of the royal family thought it best to 'anglicise' their German-sounding names. Saxe-Coburg-Gotha abruptly became the house of Windsor. George did his best to keep up public morale during the horrific carnage through visits to military hospitals and to the troops in France. George maintained a reserved dignity without critical comment, though he surely must have had thoughts as to the conduct of his government and the military that oversaw the death of nearly 1 million British subjects. George later laid the blame for the catastrophic slaughter on his German cousin, Kaiser Wilhelm II.

While the war was in progress George missed an opportunity for Britain to rescue his Russian cousin, Czar Nicholas II and his family, following the abdication of Nicholas and the subsequent Bolshevik Revolution, which would lead to the murder of Nicholas and his entire family. George always deeply regretted his failure to save the Czar and his family, but later documents have suggested that it was George himself who rejected granting asylum to the Russian royal refugees for fear of later international repercussions to the United Kingdom.

George represented continuity, stability and maturity throughout the turbulent 1920s and 1930s as the UK saw Ireland granted independence, the first Labour government installed under Ramsay MacDonald, and the Great Depression begin. With Europe undecided over confrontation with the forces of Nazi Germany, Britain celebrated George's Silver Jubilee in 1935. George was already in very poor health; he had always suffered from bronchial congestion and his heavy smoking only exacerbated his condition. He was very concerned over the behaviour and future of his eldest son, Edward, Prince of Wales, and his anxieties were to be proven correct. He needn't have worried, for his second son, another George, would prove to be an admirable monarch under the crises and challenges of the Second World War.

George V died in 1936 at his favourite country estate of Sandringham. He was buried in St George's Chapel at Windsor Castle.

94. George V as a child.

EDWARD VIII

Born:	23 June 1894
Died:	28 May 1972
Reigned:	1936
Parents:	George, Duke of York (later George V), and Princess Mary of Teck (later Queen Mary)
Married:	Mrs Bessie Wallis (Warfield) Simpson
Children:	None
House:	Windsor
Illustration:	95. Edward VIII on holiday

Edward VIII succeeded his father George V in 1936 but was never crowned, choosing instead to abdicate the title to his brother George later that same year. His reason for this action was to marry a twice-divorced American woman, Wallis (Warfield) Simpson, a union that provoked what was then considered to be a constitutional crisis. Whether or not this marriage would have been accepted by Parliament and the public remains conjecture, although there has always been sentiment to the belief that Edward did not truly wish to be king and that this controversy allowed him to bow out.

Edward VIII, always known in his family as David, had been a model Prince of Wales. Handsome, charming, and worldly, he ran in a fast set that was comfortable travelling the world while mixing with international celebrities of all types. He had longed to take a more active role in the First World War and serve at the front, but his father refused. Edward disagreed with his father over many issues, but mainly over his freewheeling lifestyle, reminiscent of that of Edward VII. The more Edward rebelled, the less responsibility his father entrusted him with. Not that Edward had any great desire to engage in domestic or foreign affairs – he was basically uninterested. He was also naïve; his comments and visits to Nazi Germany before the Second World War displayed a grave lack of political acumen and common sense. Rumours of his sympathies with the Nazi Germans, though unfounded, tarnished much of his already damaged reputation. During the Second World War he was made Governor of the Bahamas, as much to keep him out of the limelight as to give him a task.

Created Duke of Windsor in 1937, he and his wife spent the rest of their lives as international jet-setters, living mainly in France. In an act of reconciliation, his niece Queen Elizabeth II visited him shortly before he died of cancer in 1972. He is buried at Frogmore, near Windsor Castle. His wife died in 1986 and is buried beside him.

GEORGE VI

Born:	14 December 1895
Died:	6 February 1952
Reigned:	1936–1952
Parents:	George, Duke of York (later George V), and Princess Mary of Teck (later Queen Mary)
Married:	Elizabeth Bowes-Lyons
Children:	Elizabeth II and Margaret
House:	Windsor
Illustration:	96. George VI with his family

As the second son of George V and younger brother of the popular and debonair Edward, Prince of Wales, George, Duke of York, never expected to be king. Nor did he ever desire the position. To further complicate matters, the preparation to be king was short, as there was barely six months between Edward VIII's abdication and George's coronation at Westminster Abbey in May of 1937. It was an anxious moment for the naturally shy and retiring forty-one-year-old father of two, who was already extremely nervous about his ability to speak in public due to a pronounced speech impediment. But George, or 'Bertie' as he was referred to by his family, never lacked for courage, and he worked diligently to overcome his stammer to the point of being able to speak on the radio and at public functions with some degree of confidence. George was to prove himself a worthy monarch of great distinction during the Second World War, displaying a unifying example of courage and fortitude by remaining in London during the Blitz.

As the second son to a king, similar to both William IV and his father George V, George entered the Royal Navy in 1913 as a midshipman and served during the First World War, showing his mettle with distinguished service at the famous Battle of Jutland in 1916. George was comfortable in the Navy and felt secure in the disciplined life of a sailor, even though he suffered from seasickness and gastric ailments.

George's marriage to Elizabeth Bowes-Lyons, a lady who would go on to become a legend in her own right, proved to be a happy and successful union. The family refused to leave London during the war, and did much to raise morale by their continued presence in the bomb-weary capital during the darkest days when Britain stood alone against Nazi Germany. Both of their daughters served in uniform, and much admiration and respect for the monarchy was re-established.

After the war George witnessed the dismembering of the British Empire and the United Kingdom's struggle with a collapsed post-war economy. A heavy smoker, George's always fragile health suffered a serious blow with the discovery of lung cancer. He died in 1952 and was buried at St George's Chapel in Windsor Castle. His courage and resoluteness, coupled with his genuine humility, gave him a most special place in the hearts of his countrymen.

ELIZABETH II

Born:	21 April 1926
Reigned:	1952–
Parents:	George VI and Elizabeth Bowes-Lyon
Married:	Philip, Duke of Edinburgh; son of Prince Andrew of Greece and Princess Alice (great-granddaughter of Queen Victoria)
Children:	Three sons: Charles, Prince of Wales, Andrew and Edward. One daughter: Anne
House:	Windsor
Illustration:	97. Elizabeth II

One of the longest-reigning of England's monarchs, Elizabeth II has earned a fond spot in the hearts of her nation's subjects through determined devotion and dedication to duty. Born in 1926 to the Duke of York, Elizabeth became heiress presumptive in 1936 when her father unexpectedly became king upon the abdication of Edward VIII. Elizabeth succeeded her father as monarch in 1952 and has now reigned for over sixty years. She has brought grace, dignity, and a touch of informality to the royal presence, and in keeping with the gradual diminishing of royal prerogatives, now pays income tax. Her long and healthy life has backed up the line of succession several generations so that behind Elizabeth waits her son Charles, who will be followed by his son William, who in turn will be followed by his son George.

During the Second World War, Elizabeth was not allowed to serve as a nurse but was permitted to join the Auxiliary Training Service to drive heavy vehicles. After the war she toured various parts of the world with her parents in preparation for her future as queen. In 1947 she wed Prince Philip of Greece and Denmark, who renounced his titles and took the surname of his mother, Mountbatten. Both Elizabeth and Philip were great-great-grandchildren of Queen Victoria. They went on to have three sons and a daughter.

Elizabeth was on tour in Kenya when she learned of her father's death in February 1952. She was officially crowned at Westminster Abbey in June 1953. Since then she has made numerous tours around the world as the United Kingdom's head of state, and has made visiting the Commonwealth nations a regular feature. She is probably the most widely travelled head of state in history.

Elizabeth has overcome difficult situations in both her family and her royal situation. The circus-like sideshow of the marital problems and subsequent divorces of her sons Charles and Andrew from their respective wives, and the tragic death of Charles's ex-wife Diana Spencer in a Paris automobile accident, cast long shadows and many questions on the royal family's viability in today's world. The outpouring of public sorrow at Diana's death brought home the depth of grief the nation felt. It also served as a powerful reminder to the royal household of the need to connect on a more personal level with their subjects.

The excitement of Prince William's 2011 marriage to Kate Middleton, the 2013 birth of their son George, and the queen's Jubilees celebrated in 2002 and 2012 have all helped to restore and renew a joy and a common heritage to the nation. It has not only been 1,000 years of monarchs, but over 1,000 years of shared history – symbolised in the royal monarchy of the United Kingdom.

98. George VI, the Queen Mother, the future Elizabeth II and Princess Margaret in a stained-glass window in Canterbury Cathedral.

66

THE HEIRS

CHARLES, PRINCE OF WALES

Born:	14 November 1948
Parents:	Prince Philip Mountbatten, Duke of Edinburgh, and Elizabeth II
Married:	(1.) Diana Spencer (2.) Camilla (*née* Shand) Parker Bowles
Children:	(1.) Two sons: William and Harry
Illustration:	99. Charles, Prince of Wales

What will happen when the long reign of Elizabeth II comes to an end? Most assume that Charles, Prince of Wales, will succeed to the throne, since he is by birth the next in line. The alternative would be for Charles to decline and make way for his eldest son William, Duke of Cambridge. There is also the possibility that the United Kingdom could abandon its monarchy, do away with a heritage dating back more than 1,000 years, and dispense with a royal head of state. However, given the excitement, enthusiasm, and positive publicity for the recent marriage of Prince William to Catherine Middleton in 2011, followed by the birth of their first son, George, in 2013, it seems doubtful that the UK is willing or eager to jettison its royal tradition. Quite the reverse; public opinion polls show the monarchy to be currently quite popular, and although the cost for royal upkeep is expensive, there are also undeniable economic benefits from the enormous tourist interest in the trappings of the royal family and its colourful pageantry.

Charles's career as the long-running Prince of Wales has had its ups and downs. A graduate of Trinity College, Cambridge, Charles served in the Royal Navy (1971–1976), and is a trained pilot. In 1981 he had a celebrated marriage to Diana Spencer that produced two sons. This union ended in a scandalous divorce, featuring extramarital affairs on the parts of both partners. They were divorced in 1996. Diana's shocking and violent death in 1997, in an automobile accident, brought a tragic end to this one-time fairy-tale romance. Charles married Camilla Parker Bowles in 2005.

Charles has written several books and has been an outspoken critic on subjects ranging from urban architecture to the dangers posed by climate change. His Prince's Trust charity, founded in 1976, along with several others of his charitable organisations, claims to be the largest charitable foundation in the UK. Charles is now the longest-serving heir to the throne in British royal history, having been on deck since 1952.

WILLIAM, DUKE OF CAMBRIDGE
Born: 21 June 1982
Parents: Charles, Prince of Wales, and Diana Spencer
Married: Catherine Middleton
Children: One son, George
Illustration: 100. William, Duke of Cambridge

Charles's eldest son is William, Duke of Cambridge. William is a graduate of the University of St Andrews and has served in the royal military since 2005. Like his father before him, he is a trained pilot. He married Catherine Middleton in 2011, a marriage that has already produced one son, George, born in 2013. Therefore, there are now three generations of male heirs backed up in line behind Elizabeth.

GEORGE, PRINCE OF CAMBRIDGE
Born: 22 July 2013
Parents: William, Duke of Cambridge, and Catherine Middleton

William's marriage has generated a great deal of positive enthusiasm for the monarchy. There is also considerable speculation on the intent of Charles concerning his assumption of the crown. Whatever the eventual outcome, the sitting monarch at this point in time remains the United Kingdom's official head of state, and the focal point of much media attention. Whoever becomes the next monarch will be inheriting the responsibility of a 1,000-year-old tradition, but, perhaps more importantly, he will also be accepting the challenge to provide a meaningful purpose to not only his own reign, but to the future of the position of the monarchy itself.

PLACES TO VISIT

Palaces, castles, and cathedrals with rich connections to the royal kings and queens of England. Most are open to the public, although some have limited opening times and dates.

1. The Tower of London, London.
2. Buckingham Palace, London.
3. St James's Palace, London.
4. The Banqueting House, London.
5. Kensington Palace, London.
6. Westminster Abbey, London.
7. St Paul's Cathedral, London.
8. Hampton Court Palace, East Molesey, Surrey.
9. Windsor Castle, Windsor, Berkshire.
10. Kew Palace and Gardens, Richmond, Surrey.
11. The Royal Pavilion, Brighton, East Sussex.
12. Palace of Holyroodhouse, Edinburgh, Scotland.
13. Edinburgh Castle, Edinburgh, Scotland.
14. Caernarfon Castle, Caernarfon, Wales.
15. Osborne House, East Cowes, Isle of Wight.

101. St George's Chapel, Windsor Castle, Berkshire.

IMAGE CREDITS

1. Yale Center for British Art, Paul Mellon Collection.
2. Jonathan Reeve, JR951b53p505 15001550.
3. Jonathan Reeve, JRb12p129 9501000.
4. Jonathan Reeve, JRb12fp90.
5. Elizabeth Norton.
6. Photograph by Adrian Pingstone, public domain.
7 Elizabeth Norton.
8. Elizabeth Norton.
9. Elizabeth Norton.
10. Elizabeth Norton.
11. Elizabeth Norton.
12. Jonathan Reeve, JRb18p9.
13. Elizabeth Norton.
14. Elizabeth Norton.
15. Jonathan Reeve, JRb12p145 10001050.
16. Christina Rex.
17. Jonathan Reeve, JR1117slide 10001100.
18. The City of Bayeux.
19. The City of Bayeux.
20. The City of Bayeux.
21. Stephen Porter.
22. Stephen Porter.
23. Stephen Porter.
24. Jonathan Reeve, JR775b58fp14c.
25. Elizabeth Norton.
26. Stephen Porter.
27. Stephen Porter.
28. Stephen Porter.
29. Jonathan Reeve, JR2222b99plateXIX 11001200.
30. Jonathan Reeve, JRb18p2.
31. Library of Congress.
32. Jonathan Reeve, JRb18p5L.
33. David Sawtell via Elizabeth Norton.
34. Ripon Cathedral.
35. Jonathan Reeve, JR718b18p204 13001350.
36. Jonathan Reeve, JRb11fp414.
37. Jonathan Reeve JR 2152b97plate22 13501400.

38. Elizabeth Norton.
39. David Sawtell via Elizabeth Norton.
40. Ripon Cathedral.
41. Jonathan Reeve, JR1729b90fp85 14001500.
42. Jonathan Reeve, JR1561folio6 14001450.
43. Yale Center for British Art.
44. Ripon Cathedral.
45. David Baldwin.
46. Ripon Cathedral.
47. Yale University Art Gallery, Edwin Austin Abbey Memorial Collection.
48. Jonathan Reeve, JR1731b90fp109C 14001500.
49. Yale Center for British Art.
50. Elizabeth Norton.
51. Amanda Miller at Amanda's Arcadia. Thanks also to the Reverend Canon of Leicestershire.
52. Elizabeth Norton.
53. Yale Center for British Art, Paul Mellon Collection.
54. Stephen Porter.
55. Ripon Cathedral.
56. Jonathan Reeve, JRpc219 15001550.
57. Elizabeth Norton.
58. Elizabeth Norton.
59. Stephen Porter.
60. Elizabeth Norton.
61. Ripon Cathedral.
62. Ripon Cathedral.
63. Jonathan Reeve, JRCD2b20p1004 15001600.
64. Jonathan Reeve, JR1719b89fpiii 16001700.
65. Jonathan Reeve, JR1003b66fp112 15001600.
66. Jonathan Reeve JR1009b66p181 15001600.
67. Jonathan Reeve, JR1168b4fp747 15501600.
68. Yale Center for British Art.
69. Ripon Cathedral.

70. Jonathan Reeve, JR1722f16 16001700.
71. National Gallery of Art, Washington, Samuel H. Kress Collection.
72. Jonathan Reeve, JR296b10p1204 16501700.
73. Yale Center for British Art.
74. Jonathan Reeve, JR1900b94frontis c 16501700.
75. National Gallery of Art.
76. Jonathan Reeve, JR1959b24p1440 16501700.
77. Yale Center for British Art.
78. Yale Center for British Art.
79. Yale Center for British Art.
80. Jonathan Reeve, JR1960b24p1488 16501700.
81. Jonathan Reeve, JR1905b94fp160 16501700.
82. Elizabeth Norton.
83. Yale Center for British Art.
84. Rijks museum.
85. Yale Center for British Art.
86. Yale Center for British Art, Paul Mellon Collection.
87. Yale Center for British Art, Paul Mellon Collection.
88. Library of Congress.
89. Jonathan Reeve, JRb96p1510.
90. National Gallery of Art, Washington.
91. Library of Congress.
92. Library of Congress.
93. Library of Congress.
94. Library of Congress.
95. National Media Bureau, USA.
96. Jonathan Reeve, JR1722b90fp304 19002000.
97. NASA.
98. Amy Licence.
99. Department of Defense, USA.
100. Department of Defense, USA.
101. Robert Parker.

FURTHER READING

Ashley, Mike, *British Kings and Queens* (Robinson Publishing, 1998).

Cannon, John and Ralph Griffiths, *The Oxford Illustrated History of the British Monarchy* (Oxford University Press, 1988).

Cawthorne, Nigel, *Kings and Queens of England* (Arcturus Publishing Limited, 2009).

Clayton, Hugh, *Royal Faces: 900 Years of British Monarchy* (Crown copyright, Her Majesty's Stationery Office, 1977).

Crofton, Ian, *The Kings and Queens of England* (Sterling Publishing, 2006).

Grant, Neil, *Kings and Queens* (Harper and Collins, 1996).

Loades, David, *The Kings & Queens of England: The Biography* (Amberley Publishing, 2013).

Parker, Robert, *British Prime Ministers* (Amberley Publishing, 2011).

Smith, Goldwin, *A History of England* (Charles Scribner's Sons, 1966).

Williamson, David, *The Kings and Queens of England* (National Portrait Gallery Publications, 1998).

ACKNOWLEDGEMENTS

No worthwhile enterprise is created in a vacuum – and this effort is no different. The crew at Amberley Publishing are remarkable for their professional approach in all matters relating to this publication and this includes but is not limited to Jonathan Reeve for his inspiration and repeated encouragement to embark on this project. I would be completely remiss without praising the tireless energies of my editor Christian Duck – her suggestions, guidance, and enthusiasm were invaluable. I would like to especially thank my dear English cousins who have treated their American cousin with such charming patience and kindness during many memorable visits to England: Gina Hilsden, Annette Wood, and Rose Taylor. And finally, my beloved wife Sheila, whose support and companionship guarantees every visit to England is a joy and a pleasure. Any errors of fact or interpretation in this book are entirely mine.

R. J. P.

More Kings & Queens of England from Amberley Publishing

THE TUDORS
Richard Rex

'The best introduction to England's most important dynasty'
DAVID STARKEY

£9.99   978-1-4456-0700-9   272 pages PB 143 illus, 66 col

RICHARD III
David Baldwin

'A believably complex Richard, neither wholly villain nor hero'
PHILIPPA GREGORY

£9.99   978-1-4456-1591-2   296 pages PB 80 illus, 60 col

KATHARINE OF ARAGON
Patrick Williams

'Williams has the courage to march in where most biographers have feared to tread'
SARAH GRISTWOOD, BBC HISTORY MAGAZINE

£25.00   978-1-84868-325-9   512 pages HB   70 col illus

WILLIAM THE CONQUEROR
Peter Rex

'Rex has a real ability to communicate difficult issues to a wide audience'
BBC HISTORY MAGAZINE

£12.99   978-1-4456-0698-9   304 pages PB 43 illus, 30 col

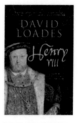

ENGLAND'S QUEENS: THE BIOGRAPHY
Elizabeth Norton

'A truly enlightening read' **THEANNEBOLEYNFILES.COM**

£16.99   978-1-4456-0904-1   432 pages PB 241 illus, 184 col

HENRY VIII
David Loades

'David Loades Tudor biographies are both highly enjoyable and instructive, the perfect combination' **ANTONIA FRASER**

£12.99   978-1-4456-0704-7   512 pages PB 113 illus, 49 col

CATHERINE PARR
Elizabeth Norton

'Norton cuts an admirably clear path through tangled Tudor intrigues'
JENNY UGLOW, THE FINANCIAL TIMES

£9.99   978-1-4456-0383-4   304 pages PB 49 illus, 39 col

ANNE BOLEYN
Lacey Baldwin Smith

'The perfect introduction'
SUZANNAH LIPSCOMB, BBC HISTORY MAGAZINE

£20.00   978-1-4456-1023-8   240 pages HB 60 illus, 40 col

THE KINGS AND QUEENS OF ENGLAND
David Loades

£25.00 978-1-4456-0582-1
512 pages HB 200 illus, 150 col

ELFRIDA
Elizabeth Norton

£20.00 978-1-4456-1486-1
224 pages HB 40 illus

ELIZABETH OF YORK
Amy Licence

£20.00 978-1-4456-0961-4
272 pages HB 40 illus, 10 col

EDWARD THE CONFESSOR
Peter Rex

£12.99 978-1-4456-0476-3
256 pages PB 30 col illus

Also available as ebooks
Available from all good bookshops or to order direct
Please call **01453-847-800 www.amberleybooks.com**